Algebra Practice

By

DR. BARBARA SANDALL, Ed.D.,
DR. MELFRIED OLSON, Ed.D.,
and TRAVIS OLSON, M.S.

COPYRIGHT © 2006 Mark Twain Media, Inc.

ISBN 10-digit: 1-58037-325-9
13-digit: 978-1-58037-325-8

Printing No. CD-404042

D1370693

Mark Twain Media, Inc., Publishers
Distributed by Carson-Dellosa Publishing LLC

The Common Core State Standards for Mathematics emphasize the importance of students being able to write and interpret numerical expressions and being able to analyze patterns and relationships. *Algebra Practice* is aligned with the Common Core State Standards for Mathematics and provides students with practice in number systems, number properties, mathematical operations, expressions, radicals, equations, rectangular coordinate systems, and functions. (See www.corestandards.org)

This product has been correlated to state, national, and Canadian provincial standards. Visit www.carsondellosa.com to search and view its correlations to your standards.

Table of Contents

Table of Contents (cont.)

Introduction to the *Math Practice* Series

The *Math Practice series* will introduce students in middle school and high school to the course topics of Pre-Algebra, Algebra, Algebra II, and Geometry. All of the practice books are aligned with the National Council of Teachers of Mathematics (NCTM) *Principles and Standards for School Mathematics*. (NCTM 2000)

This series is written for classroom teachers, parents, families, and students. The practice books in this series can be used as a full unit of study or as individual lessons to supplement textbooks or curriculum programs. Parents and students can use this series as an enhancement to what is being done in the classroom or as a tutorial at home. Students will be given a basic overview of the concepts, and examples, practice problems, and challenge problems using the concepts introduced in the section. At the end of each section, there will be a set of problems to check progress on the concepts and a challenge set of problems over the whole section. At the end of the book, there will be problems for each section that can be used for assessment.

According to the Mathematics Education Trust and NCTM, new technologies require the fundamentals of algebra and algebraic thinking as a part of the background for all citizens. These technologies also provide opportunities to generate numerical examples, graph data, analyze patterns, and make generalizations. An understanding of algebra is also important because business and industry require higher levels of thinking and problem solving. NCTM also suggests that understanding geometry, including the characteristics and properties of two- and three-dimensional shapes, spatial relationships, symmetry, and the use of visualization and spatial reasoning, can also be used in solving problems.

The NCTM *Standards* suggest that content and vocabulary are necessary, but of equal importance are the processes of mathematics. The process skills described in the *Standards* include: problem solving, reasoning, communication, and connections. The practice books in this series will address both the content and processes of algebra and algebraic thinking and geometry. This worktext, *Algebra Practice,* will help students transition from arithmetic to algebra.

Common Mathematics Symbols and Terms

Term	Symbol/Definition	Example
Addition sign	+	$2 + 2 = 4$
Subtraction sign	−	$4 - 2 = 2$
Multiplication sign	x or a dot • or 2 numbers or letters together or parenthesis	3×2 $2 • 2$ $2x$ $2(2)$
Division sign	÷ or a slash mark (/) or a horizontal fraction bar	$6 ÷ 2$ $4/2$ $\frac{4}{2}$
Equals or is equal to	=	$2 + 2 = 4$
Does Not Equal	≠	$5 ≠ 1$
Parentheses – symbol for grouping numbers	( )	$(2 \times 5) + 3 =$
Pi – a number that is approximately 22/7 or ≈ 3.14	π	$3.1415926…$
Negative number – to the left of zero on a number line	-	-3
Positive number – to the right of zero on a number line	+	$+4$
Less than	<	$2 < 4$
Greater than	>	$4 > 2$
Greater than or equal to	≥	$2 + 3 ≥ 4; 2 • 5 ≥ 10$
Less than or equal to	≤	$2 + 1 ≤ 4; 3 + 2 ≤ 5$
Is approximately	≈	$π ≈ 3.14$
Radical sign	$\sqrt{\ }$ $\sqrt[n]{\ }$ n represents the index, which is assumed to be 2, the square root, when there is none shown.	$\sqrt{9}$ The square root of 9 $\sqrt[3]{27}$ The cube root of 27
The nth power of a	a^n	$3^2 = 9$

1

Common Mathematics Symbols and Terms (cont.)

Variables	Are letters used for unknown numbers	$x + 8 = 12$ x is the letter representing the unknown number or variable
Mathematical Sentence	Contains two mathematical phrases joined by an equals (=) or an inequality $\{\neq, <, >, \leq, \geq\}$ sign	$2 + 3 = 5$ $9 - 3 > 5$ $3x + 8 = 20$ $4 + 2 \neq 5$
Equation	Mathematical sentence in which two phrases are connected with an equals (=) sign.	$5 + 7 = 12$ $3x = 12$ $1 = 1$
Mathematical Operations	Mathematics has four basic operations: addition, subtraction, multiplication, and division. Symbols are used for each operation.	+ sign indicates addition − sign indicates subtraction ÷ indicates division • or x indicates multiplication
Like Terms	Terms that contain the same variables with the same exponents and differ only in their coefficients	3, 4, 5 $3c, -5c, \frac{1}{2}c$ the variable is the same with the same exponent; they are like terms.
Unlike Terms	Terms with different variables, or terms with the same variable but different exponents	$5 + a$ Cannot be added because they are unlike terms $3x + 4y + 1z$ Cannot be added because the variables are different, so they are unlike terms
Coefficient	The number in front of the variable, that is, the numerical part of a term	$5x$ In this number, 5 is the coefficient
Identity Property of Addition	Any number or variable added to zero is that number or variable.	$0 + 5 = 5$ $-3 + 0 = -3$ $a + 0 = a$
Identity Property of Multiplication	Any number or variable times 1 is equal to that number or variable.	$12 \cdot 1 = 12$ $b \cdot 1 = b$ $3y \cdot 1 = 3y$

Common Mathematics Symbols and Terms (cont.)

Commutative Property of Addition	No matter the order in which you add two numbers, the sum is always the same.	$4 + 7 = 7 + 4$ $b + c = c + b$
Commutative Property of Multiplication	No matter the order in which you multiply two numbers, the answer is always the same.	$20 \times \frac{1}{2} = \frac{1}{2} \times 20$ $5 \cdot 3 = 3 \cdot 5$ $a \cdot b = b \cdot a$
Associative Property of Addition	When you add three numbers together, the sum will be the same no matter how you group the numbers.	$(5 + 6) + 7 = 5 + (6 + 7)$ $(a + b) + c = a + (b + c)$
Associative Property of Multiplication	No matter how you group the numbers when you multiply, the answer will always be the same product.	$(5 \cdot 4) \cdot 8 = 5 \cdot (4 \cdot 8)$ $(a \cdot b) \cdot c = a \cdot (b \cdot c)$
Distributive Property of Multiplication Over Addition	Allows the choice of multiplication followed by addition or addition followed by multiplication.	$3(5 + 2) = 3 \cdot 5 + 3 \cdot 2$ $a(b + c) = a \cdot b + a \cdot c$
Inverse Operation	Operation that undoes another operation	Multiplication and division $5 \cdot x = 5x$ $\frac{5x}{5} = x$ Addition and Subtraction $n + 5 - 5 = n$
Reciprocal or Multiplicative Inverse Property	Two reciprocals are multiplied, and the product is 1.	For any non-zero number: Number $\times \dfrac{1}{\text{Number}} = 1$ $\dfrac{1}{\text{Number}} \times$ Number $= 1$ $a \cdot \dfrac{1}{a} = 1$ $5 \cdot \dfrac{1}{5} = 1$

Common Mathematics Symbols and Terms (cont.)

Exponents	Shorthand for repeated multiplication	$a^2 = a \cdot a$ $y^4 = y \cdot y \cdot y \cdot y$
Square Numbers	The result of multiplying a number or variable by itself	$4 \cdot 4 = 16$ $a \cdot a = a^2$
Square Roots	A square root indicated by the radical sign $\sqrt{}$ is the positive number multiplied by itself to get the radicand.	$\sqrt{9}$ What positive number multiplied by itself = 9? $3 \cdot 3 = 9$ So $\sqrt{9} = 3$
Radicand	Number under the radical	$\sqrt{9}$ 9 is the radicand
Index	Number inside the radical crook tells how many times the number must be multiplied by itself.	$\sqrt[3]{27}$ 3 is the index What number multiplied by itself 3 times equals the radicand (27)?
Numerator	Top number in a fraction	$\frac{3}{5}$ In this fraction, 3 is the numerator.
Denominator	Bottom number in a fraction	$\frac{3}{5}$ In this fraction, 5 is the denominator.
Integers	Natural numbers, their opposites, or negative numbers, and zero	Set of integers: $\{...-3,-2,-1,0,1,2,3...\}$
Additive Inverse Property of Addition	The sum of an integer and its opposite integer will always be zero.	$a + \text{-}a = 0$ $5 + \text{-}5 = 0$
Set	Specific group of numbers or objects	Set of integers: $\{...-3,-2,-1,0,1,2,3...\}$
Quadratic Formula	If trying to solve an equation of the form $ax^2 + bx + c = 0$, then $$x = \frac{\text{-}b \pm \sqrt{b^2 - 4ac}}{2a}$$	Find the two unique solutions to any quadratic equation.

Common Mathematics Symbols and Terms (cont.)

Absolute Value	The absolute value of a number can be considered as the distance between the number and zero on the number line. The absolute value of every number will be either positive or zero. Real numbers come in paired opposites, *a* and *-a*, that are the same distance from the origin but in opposite directions. 	Absolute value of *a*: $\|a\| = a$ if *a* is positive $\|a\| = a$ if *a* is negative $\|a\| = 0$ if *a* is 0 With 0 as the **origin** on the number line, the absolute value of both -3 and +3 is equal to 3, because both numbers are 3 units in distance from the origin.
Expression	Any collection of numbers, variables, or terms with grouping symbols and mathematical operators.	$-3xy$ $2ab + b$ $2z + 4c + 2 - y$ $5[(x + 3)^2 - 4b] + 2h$
Monomial Expression	A number, variable, or the product of a number and one or more variables raised to whole number powers	a $\frac{1}{2}r$ $-3xy$
Binomial Expression	Has 2 unlike terms combined by an addition or subtraction sign. Sum of number, variable, or the product of a number and one or more variables raised to whole number powers with only two terms	$2x - 9$ $2ab + b$ $x + 3$ $x - 7$
Polynomial Expression	Has 1, 2, 3, or more terms combined by an addition or subtraction sign. Sum of number, variable, or the product of a number and one or more variables raised to whole number powers	$4a + 6$ $x^2 + 5 + 5x$ $z + a + b - a$ $2z + 4c + 2 - y$

Algebra Rules

Integer Subtraction Rule	For all integers a and b, $a - b = a + \text{-}b$	$10 - 5 = 10 + (\text{-}5)$
Equal Addition Rule	If equal quantities are added to each side of the equation, it does not change the root value of the equation.	$2y - 1 = 6$ $2y - 1 + 1 = 6 + 1$
Equal Subtraction Rule	If equal quantities are subtracted from each side of the equation, it does not change the root value of the equation.	$4x + 2 = 10$ $4x + 2 - 2 = 10 - 2$
Equal Multiplication Rule	If equal quantities are multiplied times each side of the equation, it does not change the root value of the equation.	$\dfrac{x}{6} = 3$ $(6)\dfrac{x}{6} = 3(6)$
Equal Division Rule	If equal quantities are divided into each side of the equation, it does not change the root value of the equation.	$4n = 8$ $\dfrac{4n}{4} = \dfrac{8}{4}$

Chapter 1: Review of Number Systems

Basic Overview: Real Numbers

Real numbers are a combination of all the number systems. Real numbers include natural numbers, whole numbers, integers, rational numbers, and irrational numbers. Examples of real numbers could be any number.

Summary of Numbers

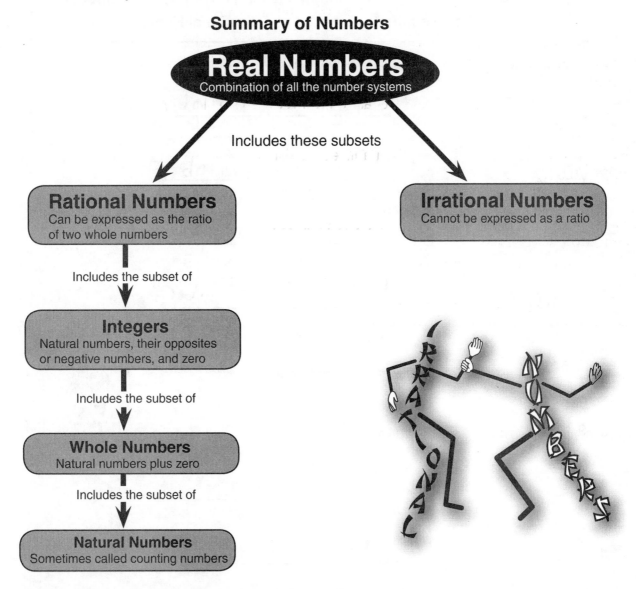

Real Numbers
Combination of all the number systems

Includes these subsets

Rational Numbers
Can be expressed as the ratio
of two whole numbers

Irrational Numbers
Cannot be expressed as a ratio

Includes the subset of

Integers
Natural numbers, their opposites
or negative numbers, and zero

Includes the subset of

Whole Numbers
Natural numbers plus zero

Includes the subset of

Natural Numbers
Sometimes called counting numbers

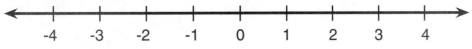

Examples of Number Systems—Real Numbers

Real numbers make up all of the numbers represented by the marks with numbers and all of the points in between the marks. Remember that the arrows indicate that this number line goes on into infinity or forever in both directions.

```
<----+----+----+----+----+----+----+----+----+---->
    -4   -3   -2   -1    0    1    2    3    4
```

Name: _____ Date: _____

Chapter 1: Review of Number Systems (cont.)

Practice: Number Systems

Directions: Using the words listed below, fill in the blanks with the correct number type(s).

Real Number	Rational Number	Integer
Whole Number	Irrational Number	

1. $\frac{1}{2}$ rational number

2. $\sqrt{0.04}$ irrational number

3. $(\sqrt{7})$ irrational number

4. 1.31313131 ...   rational number

5. -7.5   rational number

6. -9   interger

7. 5.35   rational number

8. π^2 irrational number

9. $\sqrt{81}$ Whole number

10. $\sqrt{3}$ irrational number

Name: _____ Date: _____

Chapter 1: Review of Number Systems (cont.)

11. 0.101101110111011110 ... _irrational number_

12. $\frac{2\pi}{4\pi}$ _rational number_

13. $\sqrt{0.4}$ _irrational number_

14. 0.4 • 5 _Whole number_

15. $\frac{51}{17}$ _Whole number_

Challenge Problems: Number Systems

Directions: Find values for *a* and *b* such that:

1. $\frac{a}{b}$ is an integer. _-7_

2. $\frac{a}{b}$ is undefined. _0/0_

3. $\frac{a}{b}$ is irrational. _6.235895761_

4. $\frac{a}{b}$ is zero. _0_

5. $\frac{a}{b}$ is a rational number but not an integer. _5/6_

Name: _____ Date: _____

Chapter 1: Review of Number Systems (cont.)

Checking Progress: Number Systems

Hints: "not possible" is an answer. Try solving/simplifying

Directions: Using the words listed below, fill in the blanks with the correct number type(s).

Real Number	Rational Number	Integer
Whole Number	Irrational Number	

Number   **Type or Types**

1. 0.020220222   _____

2. 4.4 ÷ 1.1   _____

3. $\sqrt{\sqrt{169}}$ _____

4. -3.222   _____

5. $1.3\overline{13}$ _____

6. $\dfrac{5.2}{0.13}$ _____

7. 5.1011011101110 …   _____

8. $\dfrac{6\pi}{5\pi}$ _____

9. $\dfrac{45\pi}{9}$ _____

10. $\sqrt{-9}$ _____

Chapter 2: Review of Properties of Numbers

Basic Overview: Properties—Identity, Commutative, Inverse, Distributive

Numbers operations have certain **properties**, or rules. The properties related to algebra include the Identity Properties, Commutative Properties, Associative Properties of Addition and Multiplication, and the Distributive Property of Multiplication Over Addition.

For any real number a, b, c:

Identity Property of Addition:	$a + 0 = a$
Identity Property of Multiplication:	$b \cdot 1 = b$
Commutative Property of Addition:	$b + c = c + b$
Commutative Property of Multiplication:	$a \cdot b = b \cdot a$
Associative Property of Addition:	$(a + b) + c = a + (b + c)$
Associative Property of Multiplication:	$(a \cdot b) \cdot c = a \cdot (b \cdot c)$
Additive Inverse Property:	$a + (-a) = 0$
Reciprocal or Multiplicative Inverse Property:	$a \cdot \dfrac{1}{a} = 1$

Distributive Property of Multiplication Over Addition:

$$a(b + c) = a \cdot b + a \cdot c$$

Examples of Properties of Numbers

Examples of Adding or Subtracting Zero From Numbers or Variables:

$a + 0 = a$

$2b - 0 = 2b$

Name: _____ Date: _____

Chapter 2: Review of Properties of Numbers (cont.)

Examples of the Identity Property of Multiplication:

$c \bullet 1 = c$

$1 \bullet (\text{-}11) = \text{-}11$

Examples of the Commutative Property of Addition:

$5 + 6 = 6 + 5$

$a + b = b + a$

Examples of the Commutative Property of Multiplication:

$20 \bullet \frac{1}{2} = \frac{1}{2} \bullet 20$

$a \bullet b = b \bullet a$

Examples of the Associative Property of Addition:

$7 + (9 + 10) = (7 + 9) + 10$

$c + (d + e) = (c + d) + e$

Name: _____ Date: _____

Chapter 2: Review of Properties of Numbers (cont.)

Examples of the Associative Property of Multiplication:

$(10 \cdot 4) \cdot 5 = 10 \cdot (4 \cdot 5)$

$(a \cdot b) \cdot c = a \cdot (b \cdot c)$

Examples of Additive Inverse Operations:

$a + (-a) = 0$

$-\sqrt{3} + \sqrt{3} = 0$

Examples of Reciprocal or Multiplicative Inverse Operations:

$\frac{3}{4}$ is the reciprocal of $\frac{4}{3}$ because $\frac{4}{3} \cdot \frac{3}{4} = 1$.

1 is its own reciprocal, and -1 is its own reciprocal.

0 has no reciprocal because division by zero is undefined.

Example of the Distributive Property of Multiplication Over Addition:

$a(b + c) = ab + ac$

$(b + c)a = ba + ca$

$4(b + 12c) = 4b + 48c$

Name: _____ Date: _____

Chapter 2: Review of Properties of Numbers (cont.)

Practice: Properties of Numbers

Directions: Identify the property being illustrated, or answer the question as posed. Choose from the properties listed in the word bank.

WORD BANK

Identity Property of Addition   Identity Property of Multiplication
Commutative Property of Addition   Commutative Property of Multiplication
Associative Property of Addition   Associative Property of Multiplication
Additive Inverse Property
Reciprocal or Multiplicative Inverse Property
Distributive Property of Multiplication Over Addition

---

1. $7 + (9 + 0) = 7 + 9$ _____

2. $13 + (5 \cdot 2) = 13 + (2 \cdot 5)$ _____

3. $13 + (5 + 2) = (13 + 5) + 2$ _____

4. $2 \cdot (9 + 3) = (2 \cdot 9) + (2 \cdot 3)$ _____

5. $(93 \cdot 5) \cdot 1 = 93 \cdot 5$ _____

6. $13 + [5 \cdot (2 \cdot 4)] = 13 + [(2 \cdot 4) \cdot 5]$ _____

7. $13 + [5 \cdot (2 \cdot 4)] = 13 + [(5 \cdot 2) \cdot 4]$ _____

8. $(13 + 4) + (9 + 2) = (9 + 2) + (13 + 4)$ _____

9. $17 + 9 - 9 = 17$ _____

Name: _____ Date: _____

Chapter 2: Review of Properties of Numbers (cont.)

10. $(41 + 4) \cdot (9 + 2) = (9 + 2) \cdot (41 + 4)$ _____

11. $(38 \cdot 4) \div 4 = 38$ _____

12. What is the reciprocal of $\frac{2}{3}$? _____

13. T or F? The reciprocal of a number is always larger than the number itself.

14. T or F? The reciprocal of 1 is 1.

15. T or F? The reciprocal of 0 is 0.

Challenge Problems: Properties of Numbers

1. T or F? By the Associative Property of Addition:

$(3 + (4 + 5)) + 6 = 3 + ((4 + 5) + 6)$

2. T or F? By the Commutative Property of Multiplication:

$3 \cdot (4 + 5) = (3 \cdot 4) + (3 \cdot 5)$

3. T or F? By the Distributive Property of Multiplication Over Addition:

$3 + (4 \cdot 5) = (3 + 4) \cdot (3 + 5)$

4. T or F? By the Distributive Property of Multiplication Over

Subtraction:

$3 \cdot (4 - 5) = (3 \cdot 4) - (3 \cdot 5)$

5. T or F? By the Identity Property of Addition:

$(3 + 1) + 1 = 3 + (1 + 1)$

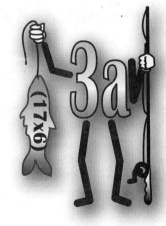

Name: _____ Date: _____

Chapter 2: Review of Properties of Numbers (cont.)

Checking Progress: Properties of Numbers

1. Use the Associative Property of Addition to mentally compute: $17 + (3 + 8)$.

   _____

2. Use the Associative Property of Multiplication to mentally compute: $(17 \cdot 2) \cdot 5$.

   _____

3. Use the Distributive Property of Multiplication Over Addition to mentally compute:

   $(17 \cdot 4) + (17 \cdot 6)$.

   _____

4. Use reciprocals to mentally compute: $\frac{4}{5} \cdot 81 \cdot \frac{5}{4}$.

   _____

In questions 5–8, use the properties of real numbers to generate a solution to each problem.

5. _____ $+ (991 \cdot 86) = (991 \cdot 86) + 221$

6. $3a + (21b \cdot 421z) = ($_____ $\cdot 421z) + 3a$

7. $39a + ($_____ $+$ _____$) = (39a + 29z) + 43a$

8. $(13a \cdot 3b) + (13a \cdot 4c) = 13a \cdot ($_____ $+$ _____$)$

9. Rewrite $513b^8 + 29b^5$ using the Distributive Property of Multiplication Over Addition.

   _____

10. Use the Associative Property to mentally compute: $(287 + 8,619) + 81$.

    _____

Name: _____ Date: _____

Chapter 3: Exponents and Exponential Expressions

Basic Overview: Exponents

Exponents are symbols that can be used as shorthand notation to indicate the action of repeated multiplication. The repeated multiplication, $2 \cdot 2 \cdot 2 \cdot 2 \cdot 2 \cdot 2 \cdot 2 \cdot 2 \cdot 2 \cdot 2 \cdot 2 \cdot 2 \cdot 2$ can be written as 2^{13} in exponential form. The square of a number means that you multiply the number by itself. The square of 5 is written as 5^2 in exponential form and is the same as $5 \cdot 5$. To get the cube of a number, multiply the number times itself three times. An example of the cube of a number is 4^3; the 4 is the **base**, and the ^{3} is the **exponent**. 4^3 is the same as $4 \cdot 4 \cdot 4$.

Examples of Exponents:

7^2 means 7 squared or 7 raised to the second power or $7 \cdot 7$.
So $7^2 = 49$

Example of Scientific Notation:

10^8 or 10 to the 8th power = 100,000,000 or $10 \cdot 10 \cdot 10 \cdot 10 \cdot 10 \cdot 10 \cdot 10 \cdot 10$

Practice: Exponents and Exponential Expressions

Directions: Evaluate each expression or answer the question posed.

1. 5^3 _____

2. $(2.1)^2$ _____

3. $5 \cdot 2^2$ _____

4. $(5 \cdot 2)^2$ _____

5. $(2b)^2$ _____

6. -3^5 _____

7. 4^5 _____

8. Which is larger? 13^2 or 2^{13} _____

9. If $5^a = 625$, then $a = ?$ _____

Name: _____ Date: _____

Chapter 3: Exponents and Exponential Expressions (cont.)

10. If $12^a = 1$, then $a = ?$ _____

11. T or F? $(-5)^4 = -5^4$ _____

12. T or F? $(-3)^5 = -3^5$ _____

13. $5^2 \cdot 2^2$ _____

14. $-10 \cdot 4^3$ _____

15. $10^3 \cdot 4$ _____

16. T or F? $4^3 \cdot 4^3 = 8^3$ _____

17. T or F? $4^3 + 4^3 = 4^6$ _____

18. T or F? $9^2 = 3^4$ _____

19. 0.1^5 _____

20. $(0.4)^5 \cdot 10^2$ _____

Challenge Problems: Exponents and Exponential Expressions

1. What is the whole-number value of a if $3^a = 800$? _____

2. For which whole-number value of a does $2^4 = 4^a$? _____

3. For what value of a does $4 \cdot 3^a = 108$? _____

4. $2 \cdot (3x) \cdot (2y) \cdot x \cdot (5y) \cdot y$ _____

5. $(0.2)^2(0.3)^3$ _____

CHALLENGE PROBLEMS EXPONENTS AND EXPONENTIAL EXPRESSIONS

5-117.) $\dfrac{200}{5} = \dfrac{5 \cdot 2^n}{5}$ Not possible,
                                        b/c 2^n will
$40 = 2^n$ never equal 40
$n = 5.322$

5-118) Yes, because x can be a decimal

5-119) a) 1: 2, 6, 10, 14, 18, 22 $t(n+1) = t(n) + 4$
         2: 24, 12, 0, -12, -24, -36 $t(n+1) = t(n) - 12$
         3: 1, 5, 9, 13, 17, 21 $t(n+1) = t(n) + 4$

      b) 1: 2, 6, 18, 54, 162, 486 $t(n+1) = t(n) \times 3$
         2: 24, 12, 6, 3, 1.5, .75 $t(n+1) = t(n)/2$
         3: 1, 5, 25, 125, 625, 3,125 $t(n+1) = t(n) \times 5$

      c) 1: 2, 6, 14, 30, 62, 126, 254 $t(n+1) = 2 \cdot t(n) + 2$
         2: 24, 12, 8, 6.67, 6.22, 6.07 $t(n+1) = t(n)/3 + 4$
         3: 1, 5, 24, 173, 1043, 6,263 $t(n+1) = 6t(n) - 1$

5-120) a) $1 + 1 - 6 = -4$ b) $-1 + 1 + 6 = 6$ c) $-8 + 4 + 12 = 8$
       d) $1000 + 100 - 60 = 1040$ e) $x = 0$
         $x^3 + x^2 - 6x + x^2 - x + 3$
         $\boxed{x^3 - 7x + 3}$

5-121) a) $23,500 \, (.85)^{15} = \$2052.82$
       b) $14,365.112 \cdot (1.12)^{20} = 138570081$

5-122) $(1056 - 116)/5 = -188$
       $1056 = -188n + x$
       $f(n) = -188n + 2560$

5-123) a) all #s
       b) whole numbers
       c) $x \neq 0$
       d) whole #s

Pg 10

1) irrational
2) whole
3) irrational
4) rational
5) rational
6) whole
7) irrational
8) rational
9) irrational
10) not possible

Pg 17

1) 125
2) 4.41
3) 20
4) 100
5) 46^2
6) -243
7) 1,024
8) 2^{13}
9) a = 4

Chapter 3: Exponents and Exponential Expressions (cont.)

Basic Overview: Combining Terms—Multiplication and Division; Evaluating Exponential Expressions

Exponents are sometimes used in a combination of numbers and variables together, and these are called **algebraic expressions**. To help in simplification, there are some simple rules that are useful.

Multiplication Rule

In general, $a^m \cdot a^n = a^{m+n}$. In words, if multiplying exponential expressions with the same base, add the exponents and keep the same base.

Division Rule

In general, $a^m \div a^n = a^{m-n}$. In words, if dividing exponential expressions with the same base, subtract the exponents and keep the same base.

To divide exponential expressions with the same base, subtract the exponents and put the answer with the base number. You can divide exponential expressions with coefficients if they have the same base. Divide the coefficients, subtract the exponents, and combine the terms.

Examples of Combining Terms

Example of Multiplying Exponential Expressions With Coefficients:

$(3x^2)(5x^5) =$
$15x^7$

Example of Dividing Exponential Expressions:

$8^5 \div 8^2 =$
$8^{5-2} = 8^3 = 512$

Examples of Evaluating Expressions:

$4^5 \div 4^2 =$
$4^{5-2} = 4^3 = 64$

$\frac{4}{2}d^{-6-(-2)} = 2d^{-4}$

Chapter 3: Exponents and Exponential Expressions (cont.)

Practice: Combining Terms

Directions: Combine terms or answer the questions posed.

1. $5x^3 + 3x^3$ _____

2. $5^3 \cdot 5^4$ _____

3. $8x^3 \div 4x$ _____

4. $2^8 \div 2^3$ _____

5. $3x^2 - 9x^2$ _____

6. $8z^2 - 8z$ _____

7. $4z^3 - 2z + 8z^3 + z$ _____

8. $2^{15}x^{13} \div 2^4x^5$ _____

9. $18x^2 - (81x^2 + 27x^2)$ _____

10. $18x^2 - 81x^2 + 27x^2$ _____

11. _____ $+ 12x^2 = 83x^2$

12. If $(2)^5(2)^a = 2^{10}$, then $a =$ _____

13. If $12^{49} \div a = 12^5$, then $a =$ _____

14. $17a + 21b - 9a - 9b$ _____

Name: _____ Date: _____

Chapter 3: Exponents and Exponential Expressions (cont.)

15. $4^2z - 2^2z$ _____

16. $(4)^{12}(7)^5 \div (4)^3(7)^2$ _____

17. Brianna thought that the following was a correct way to combine the terms, $2z^3 + 3z^5 = 5z^8$. Do you think she is correct? _____

18. $13z^5 - 19z^5$ _____

19. z^5z^{14} _____

20. $z^{14} \div z^5$ _____

Challenge Problems: Combining Terms

1. $3^2x + 5^2x$ _____

2. Suki thought $8z^3 + 8z^3 = 16z^6$. What do you think? _____

   _____

3. Lem thought that $48^5 \div 48^4 = 1$. What do you think? _____

   _____

4. $43x^5 +$ _____ $= 28x^5$

5. Judd thought that $z^5 + z^5 + z^5 = 3z^5$,

   while Mark thought that $z^5 + z^5 + z^5 = 3z^{15}$.

   Who do you think is correct?

   _____

Chapter 3: Exponents and Exponential Expressions (cont.)

Basic Overview: Raising to a Power and Negative Exponents

Consider how to handle $(3^3)^2$. Recall the meaning of 3^3, namely that $3^3 = 3 \bullet 3 \bullet 3$. This gives the result that $(3^3)^2 = (3 \bullet 3 \bullet 3)^2$. Raising the inside to the second power means to take what is inside the parentheses and multiply it by itself. Note that in the equation below, the new simplified exponent is 6. Therefore, when raising a power to a power, multiply the exponents: $(3^3)^2 = (3 \bullet 3 \bullet 3)^2 = (3 \bullet 3 \bullet 3)(3 \bullet 3 \bullet 3) = 3 \bullet 3 \bullet 3 \bullet 3 \bullet 3 \bullet 3 = 3^6$.

To solve problems with negative exponents, first find the reciprocal of the base. Finding the **reciprocal** of a number simply requires interchanging the numerator and the denominator. Change the negative exponent to a positive exponent after replacing the base with its reciprocal.

Fractional exponents can be changed into radical expressions. The numerator of the fractional exponent is the power of the number under the radical sign, and the denominator designates the index, or root.

Examples of Raising to a Power and Negative Exponents

Raising to the Zero Power:

$a^0 = 1$. Any base raised to the zero power is 1.

Power to a Power Rule:

In general, $(a^m)^n = a^{m \bullet n}$. In words, to raise a power to a power, multiply the exponents.

$(2^2)^5$

Multiply the exponents: $2 \bullet 5 = 10$

$(2^2)^5 = 2^{2 \bullet 5} = 2^{10} = 1{,}024$

Examples of Reciprocals:

The reciprocal of $\frac{1}{2}$ is $\frac{2}{1}$.

The reciprocal of $\frac{a}{b}$ is $\frac{b}{a}$.

Name: _____ Date: _____

Chapter 3: Exponents and Exponential Expressions (cont.)

Example of Solving Problems With Negative Exponents:

$$5^{-2} = \left(\frac{5}{1}\right)^{-2} = \left(\frac{1}{5}\right)^{2} = \frac{1^2}{5^2} = \frac{1}{25}$$

Example of Fractional Exponents as Radical Expressions:

$$y^{\frac{2}{3}} = \sqrt[3]{y^2}$$

Practice: Raising to a Power and Negative Exponents

Directions: Write all expressions with positive exponents.

1. $(7^5)^2$ _____

2. $(7^2)^5$ _____

3. $(x^2)^{15}$ _____

4. 3^{-4} _____

5. $(3^4)^{-2}$ _____

6. $(3^{-4})^{-2}$ _____

7. $(3^{-8})^0$ _____

8. $\left(\frac{1}{3}\right)^4$ _____

9. 2^{-5} _____

10. $\left(\frac{1}{3}\right)^{-4}$ _____

Chapter 3: Exponents and Exponential Expressions (cont.)

11. $[(3^2)^3]^2$ _____

12. 9^{-2} _____

13. T or F? $7^{-2} = (-7)^2$

14. If $(x^2)^3 = 1$, then $x =$ _____.

15. If $53^x = 1$, then $x =$ _____.

Challenge Problems: Raising to a Power and Negative Exponents

1. T or F? $5^4 = \left(\frac{1}{5}\right)^{-4}$

2. Addie thought that a^{-2} would always be a negative number. Is she correct?

   _____

3. T or F? $[(2^5)^2]^3 = 2^{10}$

4. Is there a value for a that would make a^{-4} a whole number? _____

5. Fred thought that a number with a larger exponent would always be greater than a number with a smaller exponent. Frank disagreed. Who do you think is correct?

   _____

Name: _____ Date: _____

Chapter 3: Exponents and Exponential Expressions (cont.)

Checking Progress: Exponents and Exponential Expressions

1. Evaluate. 0.02^3 _____

2. Evaluate. -4^3 _____

3. Name the largest integer value for b so that $4^b < 2,000$. _____

4. Evaluate. $12^3 \cdot 10^3$ _____

5. Evaluate. $-(3 \cdot -4)^2$ _____

6. Combine terms. $41a^2 - [(3b^4 - 7a^2) - 34b^4]$ _____

7. Combine terms. $41a^2 - [(3b^4 - 7a^2) - 34b^4]$ _____

8. Combine terms. $a^3 \cdot b^5 \cdot b^{23} \cdot a^{14} \cdot b^6$ _____

9. Rewrite $(-2)^{-2}$ using only positive exponents. The value is _____.

10. Simplify the exponent. $[(y^2)^{21}]^5$ _____

Name: _____ Date: _____

Chapter 4: Roots and Radical Expressions

Basic Overview: Square, Cube, and Higher Roots and Negative Radicands

The **principal square root** of a given number is found by determining which positive number, when multiplied by itself, is equal to the given number. The symbol $\sqrt{}$ is called a **radical sign**, and the given number inside the radical sign for which the square root is being calculated, is called the **radicand**. Another part of a radical expression is the small number in the crook outside the radical sign called the index. The **index** tells the "root" of the expression. Square roots have an index of 2, which is generally not written. The symbol for indicating a cube root is $\sqrt[3]{}$, or the third root. The cube root is the number, that when cubed, is equal to the radicand.

When there are negative radicands, the possibility of a solution is determined by whether the index is odd or even. If the index is an even number, including the number 2, a real solution cannot be computed for a negative radicand. If the index is odd and the radicand is a negative number, then the root is also a negative number. Remember, radical expressions with negative radicands can only be solved if the index is an odd number.

Examples of Square, Cube, and Higher Roots and Negative Radicands

Example of a Square Root:

$\sqrt{81}$ symbolizes the square root of 81.

What number times itself = 81?

$9 \cdot 9 = 81$

Therefore, $\sqrt{81} = 9$; the square root of 81 equals 9.

Example of a Cube Root:

$\sqrt[3]{64}$ What number multiplied by itself 3 times is equal to 64?

$4 \cdot 4 \cdot 4 = 64$

Therefore, $\sqrt[3]{64} = 4$; the cube root of 64 equals 4.

Example of a Root and Radical Greater Than 2 or 3:

$\sqrt[4]{16}$ The index is 4, so what number multiplied by itself 4 times is equal to 16?

$2 \cdot 2 \cdot 2 \cdot 2 = 2^4 = 16$.

Therefore, $\sqrt[4]{16} = 2$; the fourth root of 16 equals 2.

Name: _____ Date: _____

Chapter 4: Roots and Radical Expressions (cont.)

Example of a Radical Expression With a Negative Radicand That Can Be Solved:

$\sqrt[5]{-32}$ = -2 because $(-2)^5$ = -32.

Examples of a Radical Expression With a Negative Radicand That Cannot Be Solved:

$\sqrt[4]{-32}$

The index is even, so it cannot be solved.

Practice: Square, Cube, and Higher Roots and Negative Radicands

Directions: Simplify.

1. $\sqrt[3]{16}$ _____

2. $\sqrt[3]{125}$ _____

3. $\sqrt[20]{1}$ _____

4. $\sqrt[5]{729}$ _____

5. $\sqrt[4]{48}$ _____

6. $\sqrt[3]{4^{11}}$ _____

7. $\sqrt{-81}$ _____

8. $\sqrt[3]{-27}$ _____

9. $\sqrt[5]{-1}$ _____

Name: _____ Date: _____

Chapter 4: Roots and Radical Expressions (cont.)

10. $\sqrt[4]{-1}$ _____

11. $\sqrt[5]{-243}$ _____

12. $\sqrt[3]{\dfrac{-27}{125}}$ _____

Challenge Problems: Square, Cube, and Higher Roots and Negative Radicands

1. Fred thought that $\sqrt[40]{1} > \sqrt[5]{1}$ because 40 > 5. Ted thought that $\sqrt[40]{1} < \sqrt[5]{1}$ because 40 > 5. Who is correct? _____

2. Helene thought that if b is odd and $a > 0$, then the $\sqrt[b]{a}$ could always be found. What do you think? _____

3. T or F? $\sqrt[3]{\dfrac{-27}{125}} = \sqrt[3]{\dfrac{27}{-125}}$

Chapter 4: Roots and Radical Expressions (cont.)

Basic Overview: Simplifying Radical Expressions

Rules for Simplifying Radical Expressions

- The product of the square roots of two non-negative numbers is equal to the square root of the product of the two numbers. In symbols: $\sqrt{a} \cdot \sqrt{b} = \sqrt{a \cdot b}$

- The product of the cube roots of two numbers is equal to the cube root of the product of the two numbers. In symbols: $\sqrt[3]{a} \cdot \sqrt[3]{b} = \sqrt[3]{a \cdot b}$

- The quotient of the square roots of two numbers is equal to the square root of the quotient of the two numbers. In symbols: $\dfrac{\sqrt{a}}{\sqrt{b}} = \sqrt{\dfrac{a}{b}}$

- Multiplying both the numerator and denominator of a radicand by the same number does not change the value of the radicand.

- Radical expressions can be added and subtracted if each index is the same and the radicands are equal.

- Radical expressions can be written in exponential form using the following rule: $\sqrt[n]{a^m} = a^{\frac{m}{n}}$

- Radical expressions are not in simplified form if there is a radical in the denominator.

Examples of the Rules for Simplifying Radical Expressions

Example of Two Numbers Multiplied Under the Same Radical Sign With Two Expressions Separated:

$\sqrt{4 \cdot 9} =$

$\sqrt{4} \cdot \sqrt{9} =$

$2 \cdot 3 = 6$

Therefore, $\sqrt{4 \cdot 9} = 6$

Chapter 4: Roots and Radical Expressions (cont.)

Example of Two Radical Expressions Multiplied Together and Written as Products Under the Same Radical Sign:

$\sqrt{3} \cdot \sqrt{27} =$

$\sqrt{3 \cdot 27} = \sqrt{81}$

The square root of 81 equals 9.

Therefore, $\sqrt{3} \cdot \sqrt{27} = 9$

Example of Finding Factors for the Number Under the Radical and Taking the Square Root of the Factors:

$\sqrt{18} =$

$\sqrt{2 \cdot 9} =$

$\sqrt{2} \cdot \sqrt{9} =$

$\sqrt{2} \cdot (3) = 3\sqrt{2}$

Therefore, $\sqrt{18} = 3\sqrt{2}$

The square root of 2 is not a whole number. When rounding it to the nearest thousandth, it is ≈ 1.414.

$\sqrt{(2)(9)} \approx 3 \cdot 1.414$. Note that this is $\approx$, and not =, because the number has been rounded.

$\sqrt{(2)(9)} \approx 4.2426$

Chapter 4: Roots and Radical Expressions (cont.)

Example of Two Numbers Divided Under a Radical Sign:

$$\sqrt{\frac{9}{4}}$$

$$\frac{\sqrt{9}}{\sqrt{4}}$$

$$\sqrt{9} = 3 \qquad \sqrt{4} = 2$$

$$\sqrt{\frac{9}{4}} = \frac{3}{2}$$

Example of Multiplying the Numerator and Denominator by the Same Number:

$$\frac{5}{\sqrt{3}} =$$

$$\left(\frac{5}{\sqrt{3}}\right)\left(\frac{\sqrt{3}}{\sqrt{3}}\right) =$$

$$\left(\frac{5}{\sqrt{3}}\right)\left(\frac{\sqrt{3}}{\sqrt{3}}\right) = \frac{5\sqrt{3}}{\sqrt{3}\,(3)} = \frac{5\sqrt{3}}{\sqrt{9}}$$

$$\frac{5}{\sqrt{3}} = \frac{5\sqrt{3}}{\sqrt{9}} = \frac{5\sqrt{3}}{3}$$

Example of Addition and Subtraction of Radicals:

$$3\sqrt{5} + 4\sqrt{5} =$$

$$(3 + 4) \cdot \sqrt{5} = 7\sqrt{5}$$

$$3\sqrt[3]{x} - \sqrt[3]{x} =$$

$$(3 - 1) \cdot \sqrt[3]{x} = 2\sqrt[3]{x}$$

Name: _____ Date: _____

Chapter 4: Roots and Radical Expressions (cont.)

Practice 1: Simplifying Radical Expressions

Directions: Simplify. Assume that all variables are non-negative.

1. $\sqrt{16}$ _____

2. $\sqrt{1,600}$ _____

3. $\sqrt{(16)(25)}$ _____

4. $\sqrt{y^8}$ _____

5. $(\sqrt{y^2})(\sqrt{y^2})(\sqrt{y})(\sqrt{y})$ _____

6. $\sqrt{5} \cdot \sqrt{20}$ _____

7. $\sqrt{5} \cdot \sqrt{3}$ _____

8. If $\sqrt{19} \cdot \sqrt{a} = 38$, then $a =$ _____

9. $\sqrt{y^9}$ _____

10. $\sqrt{48}$ _____

Name: _____ Date: _____

Chapter 4: Roots and Radical Expressions (cont.)

11. $(\sqrt{48})(\sqrt{15})(\sqrt{5})$ _____

12. $\sqrt{81 \cdot 144}$ _____

13. $\sqrt{\dfrac{36}{49}}$ _____

14. $\sqrt{\dfrac{52}{3}}$ _____

15. $\sqrt{0.001}$ _____

16. $\sqrt{0.01}$ _____

17. $\sqrt{3} \cdot \sqrt{6} \cdot \sqrt{8}$ _____

18. $\sqrt{27}$ _____

19. $5\sqrt{3} \cdot 5\sqrt{3}$ _____

20. $3\sqrt{5} \cdot 5\sqrt{3}$ _____

Name: _____ Date: _____

Chapter 4: Roots and Radical Expressions (cont.)

Practice 2: Simplifying Radical Expressions

Directions: Combine like terms.

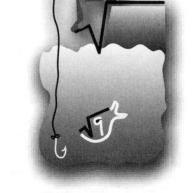

1. $5\sqrt{3} + 9\sqrt{3}$ _____

2. $9x\sqrt{5} + y\sqrt{5}$ _____

3. $6\sqrt{x^5} + 3\sqrt{x^5}$ _____

4. $41\sqrt{x} - 12\sqrt{x^4} + 9\sqrt{x} - 5\sqrt{x^4}$ _____

5. $4\sqrt{12} + 2\sqrt{3}$ _____

6. Doug computed $5\sqrt{x^4} + 6\sqrt{x^4}$ as $11x^4$. Do you agree? _____
   _____

7. Kimo thought that $\sqrt{75}$ and $25\sqrt{3}$ were the same. Do you agree? _____
   _____

8. $4\sqrt{8y} - 3\sqrt{2y}$ _____

9. $19\sqrt{5} + 3\sqrt{3} - 9\sqrt{5} - 9\sqrt{3}$ _____

10. $\sqrt{9y^4} + 9\sqrt{y^4} + y^2\sqrt{9}$ _____

11. $5\sqrt{3} + \sqrt{27} + 2\sqrt{12}$ _____

12. $5\sqrt[4]{x^5} - 2\sqrt[3]{x^5}$ _____

Name: _____ Date: _____

Chapter 4: Roots and Radical Expressions (cont.)

Challenge Problems 1: Simplifying Radical Expressions

1. Which is larger? $3\sqrt{7}$ or $7\sqrt{3}$ _____

2. Why is $\sqrt{-9}$ not -3? _____

3. If $\sqrt{15} \cdot \sqrt{a} = 5$, then what is the value of a?

   _____

4. T or F? $\sqrt{\dfrac{2}{3}} = \dfrac{1}{3}\sqrt{6}$

5. T or F? $\sqrt{\dfrac{4}{3}} = \sqrt{\sqrt{\dfrac{16}{9}}}$

Challenge Problems 2: Simplifying Radical Expressions

1. Esined thought that $6\sqrt{x^5}$ was the same as $6x^2\sqrt{x}$. Do you agree?

   _____

2. Clarice did not think that you could combine $5\sqrt{3} + 9\sqrt{3}$. Do you agree?

   _____

3. Nathan thought that $\sqrt{25+9}$ was the same as $\sqrt{25} + \sqrt{9}$. Do you agree?

   _____

Chapter 4: Roots and Radical Expressions (cont.)

Basic Overview: Fractional Roots and Radical Expressions

Radical expressions can be written as fractional exponents. The numerator is the power of the number under the radical sign, and the denominator is the number that is the index. Fractional exponents can be changed into radical expressions. The numerator is the exponent of the number under the radical sign, and the denominator is the index.

Examples of Fractional Roots and Radical Expressions

Example of a Radical Expression as a Fractional Exponent:

$$\sqrt[4]{x^3}$$

Index = 4

Exponent = 3

$$\sqrt[4]{x^3} = x^{\frac{3}{4}}$$

Example of a Fractional Exponent as a Radical Expression:

$$y^{\frac{2}{3}} =$$

$$y^{\frac{2}{3}} = \sqrt[3]{y^2}$$

Practice: Fractional Exponents and Radical Expressions

Directions: For exercises 1–6, change each to a fractional exponent.

1. $\sqrt[5]{5^3}$ _____

2. $\sqrt[3]{5^7}$ _____

3. $\sqrt{13}$ _____

Chapter 4: Roots and Radical Expressions (cont.)

4. $\sqrt[4]{a^3}$ _____

5. $\sqrt[9]{a^5}$ _____

6. $\sqrt[8]{5^7}$ _____

For exercises 7–12, change each to a radical expression.

7. $7^{\frac{1}{2}}$ _____

8. $(13y)^{\frac{1}{2}}$ _____

9. $4^{\frac{1}{2}}$ _____

10. $10^{\frac{2}{3}}$ _____

11. Which is larger? $(3 \cdot 5)^{\frac{1}{2}}$ or $3 \cdot 5^{\frac{1}{2}}$ _____

12. $17^{\frac{2}{3}}$ _____

Challenge Problems: Fractional Exponents and Radical Expressions

1. T or F? $(5 \cdot y)^{\frac{1}{2}} = 5\sqrt{y}$

2. Evelyn thought that $100^{\frac{1}{2}} = 50$, and Diane thought that $100^{\frac{1}{2}} =$ 10. With whom, if either, do you agree?

_____

_____

3. Between which two whole numbers is $10^{\frac{2}{3}}$?

_____

_____

Name: _____ Date: _____

Chapter 4: Roots and Radical Expressions (cont.)

Checking Progress: Roots and Radical Expressions

1. $\sqrt{(81)(49)}$ _____

2. $\sqrt{882}$ _____

3. $\sqrt{169z^8}$ _____

4. $a\sqrt{a^2z^7}$, $a > 0$, $z > 0$ _____

5. $\sqrt{(2^5)(5^5)(11^7)}$ _____

6. $\sqrt{63} \cdot \sqrt{14}$ _____

7. $\dfrac{\sqrt{99}}{\sqrt{45}}$ _____

8. $\dfrac{\sqrt{44}}{\sqrt{84}} \cdot \dfrac{\sqrt{35}}{\sqrt{55}}$ _____

9. $z\sqrt{2z} - \sqrt{8z^3}$ _____

10. $3\sqrt{6z^5} + 5\sqrt{150z^3}$ _____

Chapter 5: Operations

Basic Overview: Operations on Algebraic Expressions

Mathematics has four basic operations that can be performed: addition, subtraction, multiplication, and division. The operations act on terms. A **term** can be a number, a variable, or a product or quotient of numbers and variables. Determining like terms and unlike terms and the meaning of the coefficient is important to being able to work with numbers, variables, and operations.

When performing addition or subtraction, only combine like terms. When you add or subtract terms where the variables are the same, you add the **coefficients**, or the numbers in front of the variable(s). Unlike terms cannot be added. You can also subtract like terms, but you cannot subtract unlike terms. You may multiply like and unlike terms, numbers, variables, and variables with coefficients. You may divide like and unlike terms and any two numbers or any two variables. You may also divide two algebraic expressions that have both numbers and variables multiplied together.

When solving mathematical expressions that have more than one operation, it is important to do the operations in the correct order.

Order of Operations:
1. Do the operations within any parentheses first, working from innermost to outermost, using the rules below, in order.
2. Find the value of any number with an exponent.
3. Multiply and/or divide doing the operations from left to right.
4. Add and/or subtract last and do the operations from left to right.

Examples of Operations on Algebraic Expressions

Examples of Adding and Subtracting Like Terms:

$3x + 6x = 9x$

$7a - 4a = 3a$

Example of Adding Coefficients:

$\frac{1}{3}a + 4a + 7a = \frac{1}{3}a + \frac{12}{3}a + \frac{21}{3}a = \frac{34}{3}a$

Name: _____ Date: _____

Chapter 5: Operations (cont.)

Examples of Multiplying Numbers, Variables, and Coefficients:

$y \bullet y = y^2$

$5a \bullet 3b = 15ab$

Examples of Dividing Numbers, Variables, and Expressions:

$\dfrac{x}{x} = 1$

$a \div b = \dfrac{a}{b}$

$\dfrac{a}{0}$ Cannot be divided; undefined

$0 \div y = 0$ for all $y \neq 0$

Practice: Operations on Algebraic Expressions

Directions: Perform the indicated operations and combine terms.

1. $11 + 12 + 13 + 14 + 15$ _____

2. $298 + 375 - 921$ _____

3. $3a + 9b + 17c$ _____

4. $3a + 9b + 18c$ _____

5. $7.5x + 2.3x$ _____

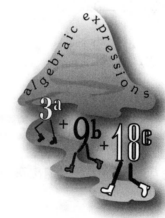

Name: _____ Date: _____

Chapter 5: Operations (cont.)

6. $(8a)(9b)$ _____

7. $\frac{5}{8} + \frac{7}{8}$ _____

8. $31x + 19x - 17a$ _____

9. $4.2 \div 0.2$ _____

10. $(17a)(5a)$ _____

11. $12a + 12b - 12c$ _____

12. $\frac{7}{2}x + \frac{21}{4}x$ _____

13. $4x - 12xy$ _____

14. $2 + \left(-\frac{21}{4}\right)$ _____

15. $8xy \cdot 7xz$ _____

16. $100y^2 + 25xy$ _____

17. $2x - (3y - 5x)$ _____

18. $2 - \left[\left(-\frac{21}{4} + 3\right) - 4\right]$ _____

19. $\dfrac{49xyz}{14xzw}$ _____

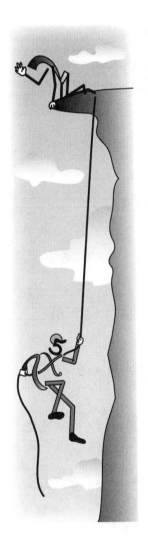

Name: _____ Date: _____

Chapter 5: Operations (cont.)

20. $\dfrac{5y^2z^4}{0.5y^3z^3}$ _____

21. $-2 - [-3 - (-5 - 9)]$ _____

22. $|5 - 9|$ _____

23. $-|5 - 9| - (-|12|)$ _____

24. $-|5 - 9| - |-12|$ _____

25. $-5 \cdot 4 \cdot -3$ _____

26. $-12 \div 4 \cdot 3 - 6$ _____

27. $-12 \div (4 \cdot 3 - 6)$ _____

28. $-12 \div [4 \cdot (3 - 6)]$ _____

29. $-|12| \div |4 \cdot (3 - 6)|$ _____

30. $42 \cdot 19^0 \cdot 5$ _____

31. $8.6 - 2.9 + 3.02$ _____

32. $8.6 - (2.9 + 3.02)$ _____

33. $3.2x + 3.2x + 3.2x + 3.2x + 3.2x = 5(\underline{\hspace{1cm}}x)$

34. $98 - 98 - 98$ _____

Name: _____ Date: _____

Chapter 5: Operations (cont.)

35. $42 \div 0$ _____

36. $42 - (0 \div 42)$ _____

37. $\frac{10}{12} \cdot \frac{15}{16} \cdot \frac{4}{5}$ _____

38. $41x + 9x - [8 \cdot (5x + 2x) - 17x]$ _____

39. $\frac{3}{5} + \frac{4}{7}$ _____

40. $5.91 \cdot 0.3$ _____

Challenge Problems: Operations on Algebraic Expressions

1. Yazier thought that $0.79 \div 0.5$ was the same as $79 \div 50$. Nozier thought that $0.79 \div 0.5$ was the same as $7.9 \div 5$. What do you think? _____

_____

2. $5^{[2-(3-4)]^2}$ _____

3. $2 - (2 - \{2 - [2 - (2 - 2)]\})$ _____

4. $2 - (-\{3 - [-(4-5)]\})$ _____

5. $11x - 3x - \{-[8 \cdot (-5x + 2x) - 17x]\}$ _____

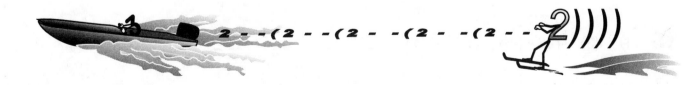

Name: _____ Date: _____

Chapter 5: Operations (cont.)

Checking Progress: Operations on Algebraic Expressions

1. $31a + 9x + 1.7y$ _____

2. $3x + 1.9x - 17y$ _____

3. $\frac{5}{2}x - \frac{21}{4}x$ _____

4. $8.1xz^2 \bullet 0.7x^2y$ _____

5. $100y^2z \div 2.5x^2y$ _____

6. $\dfrac{56xyz^2}{21x^2zw}$ _____

7. $-|0 \div 12| \div -|4 \bullet (3-6)|$ _____

8. $\dfrac{10}{1.2} \bullet \dfrac{1.5}{16} \bullet \dfrac{0.4}{0.5}$ _____

9. $\dfrac{3}{5} - \dfrac{4}{7}$ _____

10. $11x - (3x - \{-[8 \bullet (-5x + 2x)]\}) - 17x$ _____

Chapter 6: Equations and Problem Solving

Basic Overview: Equations—Linear, Quadratic, Polynomial

A **linear equation** in one variable is an equation that can be written in the general form, $ax + b = 0$, for real numbers a and b, such that $a \neq 0$. The solution of an equation is the number or numbers that make the equation true when the number is substituted for the variable. To solve an equation, it is necessary to get the variable alone on one side of the equal sign, that is, we isolate the variable. We can ensure that an equation always remains equal by doing the same operation to both sides of the equation. An equation remaining equal means that the solution isn't changed, or that the equations remain **equivalent**.

Addition Property of Equality

The same number can be added to both sides of an equation without changing the solution. Since subtraction is defined in terms of addition, ($a - b$ means $a + (-b)$), the same number can be subtracted from both sides of an equation without changing the solution.

Multiplication Property of Equality

Both sides of an equation can be multiplied by the same non-zero number without changing the solution. Since division can be defined in terms of multiplication, $\left(\dfrac{a}{b} \text{ means } a \cdot \dfrac{1}{b} \right)$, both sides of an equation can be divided by the same non-zero number without changing the solution.

When solving linear equations, use these following steps:

- Use the distributive property to remove parentheses as you employ the order of operations.
- Use the addition property to rewrite the equation with all terms containing the variable on one side, and all terms without a variable on the other side. After combining like terms, you should get an equation of the form, $ax = b$.
- Use the multiplication property to isolate the variable. This step will give a solution of the form, $x = $ some number.
- Check your solution in the original equation.

Quadratic equations are equations that contain a second-degree term and no term of higher degree. A quadratic equation can always be put into a standard form, $ax^2 + bx + c = 0$, where a, b, and c are real numbers, and $a \neq 0$.

There are several methods for solving quadratic equations, and the choice depends upon the type of quadratic equation. Consider first, the type in which $b = 0$, that is, those that have the form $ax^2 + c = 0$. Equations of this form are solved by using the **Square Root Property: For any real number k, the equation $x^2 = k$ is equivalent to $x = \pm\sqrt{k}$.** If we use our basic equation-solving steps, we end up with $x^2 = \dfrac{-c}{a}$, and applying the square root property

Chapter 6: Equations and Problem Solving (cont.)

for $k = \dfrac{-c}{a}$, yields $x = \pm\sqrt{\dfrac{-c}{a}}$. Notice that if k is negative, there are no real solutions, and if $k = 0$, there is only the one solution, $x = 0$.

Second, consider the type of quadratic equations in which $c = 0$, that is, those with the form $ax^2 + bx = 0$. Equations of this form can be factored and rewritten as $x \cdot (ax + b) = 0$. These quadratic equations can then be solved by using the **Zero-Factor Property: If A and B are algebraic expressions such that A • B = 0, then either A = 0 or B = 0.** Hence our factored form $x \cdot (ax + b) = 0$ yields the two solutions, $x = 0$ or $x = \dfrac{-b}{a}$, the latter from solving the linear equation $ax + b = 0$.

The third type of quadratic equations, for which none of the constants, a, b, or c is equal to zero, can be solved by completing the square, by factoring, which is essentially the reverse of the FOIL method, or by using the quadratic formula: $x = \dfrac{-b \pm \sqrt{b^2 - 4ac}}{2a}$

A **polynomial equation in one variable** has a single term or a finite sum of terms in which the powers of the variable are whole numbers. A polynomial equation is named for the degree of the term with the highest power of the variable. First-, second- and third-degree polynomials, are named linear, quadratic, and cubic polynomials, respectively. Polynomials with one, two, and three terms are called monomials, binomials, and trinomials, respectively.

Standard form for a polynomial equation is with a descending order of the powers of the terms on one side of the equation set equal to zero on the other side. To solve a polynomial equation, put the equation in standard form and use an appropriate factoring method. The factors may be linear or quadratic. By using the zero-product property, you can set each factor equal to zero and solve it according to the previous lessons. Check your answers in the original equation.

To solve **rational equations**, eliminate the denominators by the multiplication of each term in the equation by the least common denominator, and then solving the resulting polynomial equation. You will need to check for extraneous solutions, which are answers that do not satisfy the original equation.

Examples of Equations—Linear, Quadratic, Polynomial

Example of the Addition Property of Equality:

$x - 6 = 18$

$(x - 6) + 6 = 18 + 6$

$x + (-6 + 6) = 24$

$x = 24$

Chapter 6: Equations and Problem Solving (cont.)

Example of the Subtraction Property of Equality:

$x + 2 = 11$

$(x + 2) - 2 = 11 - 2$

$x + (2 - 2) = 9$

$x = 9$

Example of the Multiplication Property of Equality:

$\frac{1}{4}y = 5$

$4 \cdot (\frac{1}{4}y) = 4 \cdot 5$

$(4 \cdot \frac{1}{4})y = 20$

$y = 20$

Example of the Division Property of Equality:

$5a = 120$

$\frac{1}{5}(5a) = \frac{1}{5} \cdot 120$

$\frac{5a}{5} = \frac{120}{5}$

$a = 24$

Example of Applications and Problem Solving Using a Linear Equation:

LaVon received 54 points on his last test. This represented a grade of 75% for the test. How many points were on the test?

$54 = 0.75 \cdot x$

$\frac{54}{0.75} = \frac{0.75 \cdot x}{0.75}$

$72 = x$

Examples of Quadratic Equations:

$2x^2 - 3x + 1 = 0$ $-5x^2 + 7 = 0$ $\frac{1}{2}x^2 + x = 0$

Chapter 6: Equations and Problem Solving (cont.)

Example of Putting a Quadratic Equation Into Standard Form:

$a(2a + 8) = 10$

$(a \bullet 2a) + (a \bullet 8) = 10$ Distributive Property

$(2a^2 + 8a) - 10 = 10 - 10$ Addition Property of Equality

$2a^2 + 8a - 10 = 0$ Standard Form, ready to solve

Example of Putting a Quadratic Equation Into Standard Form:

$(y - 5)(y - 3) = 8$

$y^2 - 3y - 5y + 15 = 8$ FOIL Method

$y^2 - 8y + 15 = 8$ Combine like terms.

$y^2 - 8y + 15 - 8 = 8 - 8$ Subtraction Property of Equality

$y^2 - 8y + 7 = 0$ Standard Form, ready to solve

Example of Putting a Quadratic Equation Into Standard Form:

$3x^2 - 7x = 4$

$3x^2 - 7x - 4 = 4 - 4$

$3x^2 - 7x - 4 = 0$

Example of Solving a Quadratic Equation of the Form: $ax^2 + c = 0$

$2x^2 - 98 = 0$

$(2x^2 - 98) + 98 = 0 + 98$ Addition Property of Equality

$2x^2 + (-98 + 98) = 98$ Associative Property of Addition

$2x^2 = 98$

$\frac{1}{2} \bullet 2x^2 = \frac{1}{2} \bullet 98$ Multiplication Property of Equality

$x^2 = 49$ Apply the Square Root Property

$x = \pm\sqrt{49} = \pm 7$

Chapter 6: Equations and Problem Solving (cont.)

Example of Solving a Quadratic Equation of the Form: $ax^2 + bx = 0$

$x^2 + 10x = 0$ Factor an x from both terms on the left side.

$x \cdot (x + 10) = 0$ Use the Zero-Product Property.

Set both factors on the left side equal to zero and solve each linear equation:

$x = 0$ or $x + 10 = 0$

$(x + 10) - 10 = 0 - 10$

$x + (10 - 10) = -10$

$x = 0$ or $x = -10$

Example of Using Factoring Method to Solve a Quadratic Equation: $ax^2 + bx + c = 0$

$x^2 - 5x + 4 = 0$ Determine the two numbers whose sum is -5 and whose product is +4. The two numbers are -1 and -4.

$x^2 - 4x - x \cdot (x - 4) = 0$ Rewrite the middle term -5x as -4$x - x$.

$x \cdot (x - 4) - 1 \cdot (x - 4) = 0$ Factor the four terms by grouping each set of two terms.

$(x - 4) \cdot (x - 1) = 0$ Use the Zero-Product Property to solve by setting each linear factor equal to zero.

$x - 1 = 0$ or $x - 4 = 0$

$(x - 1) + 1 = 0 + 1$ $(x - 4) + 4 = 0 + 4$

$x + (-1 + 1) = 1$ $x + (-4 + 4) = 4$

$x = 1$ or $x = 4$

Chapter 6: Equations and Problem Solving (cont.)

Example of the Completing the Square Method to Solve a Quadratic Equation:

$x^2 + 2x = 1$

$x^2 + 2x + 1 = 1 + 1$ Make it look like a perfect square by adding 1 to both sides.

$x^2 + 2x + 1 = 2$

$(x + 1)^2 = 2$ Factor the equation.

$\sqrt{(x + 1)^2} = \pm\sqrt{2}$ Solution can be found by taking the square root of each side.

$x + 1 = \pm\sqrt{2}$

$(x + 1) - 1 = (\pm\sqrt{2}) - 1$

$x = -1 \pm \sqrt{2}$

$x = -1 + \sqrt{2}$ or $x = -1 - \sqrt{2}$ are the two solutions for the equation.

Example of Solving a Quadratic Equation Using the Quadratic Formula:

$6x^2 - x - 2 = 0$ $a = 6,\ b = -1,\ c = -2$

Quadratic Formula:

$$x = \frac{-b \pm \sqrt{b^2 - 4ac}}{2a} = \frac{-(-1) \pm \sqrt{(-1)^2 - 4(6)(-2)}}{2(6)} = \frac{1 \pm \sqrt{49}}{12} = \frac{1 \pm 7}{12}$$

$$x = \frac{1 + 7}{12} = \frac{8}{12} = \frac{2}{3} \quad \text{or} \quad x = \frac{1 - 7}{12} = \frac{-6}{12} = \frac{-1}{2}$$

Example of Solving Polynomial Equations Degree 3 by Factoring:

$6x^3 + 22x^2 = 8x$ Solve this cubic polynomial equation.

$ax^3 + bx^2 + cx + d = 0$ Polynomial equation in standard decreasing form.

$6x^3 + 22x^2 - 8x = 0$ Standard form, ready to be factored.

$2x \bullet (3x^2 + 11x - 4) = 0$ Common factor of $2x$ for all three terms.

$2x \bullet (3x^2 + 12x - 1x - 4) = 0$ To factor the quadratic factor, determine two numbers whose sum is +11 and whose product is $(3) \bullet (-4) = -12$. Rewrite $11x$ as $12x - 1x$.

Chapter 6: Equations and Problem Solving (cont.)

$2x \cdot [3x \cdot (x + 4) - 1 \cdot (x + 4)] = 0$ Factor by grouping: Find the common factor for each pair of terms inside the parentheses.

$2x \cdot (x + 4) \cdot (3x + 1) = 0$ Common grouping factor is $x + 4$.

Use the zero-product property to solve the three linear factors by setting each to zero.

$2x = 0$	or	$x + 4 = 0$	or	$3x - 1 = 0$
Therefore, $x = 0$	or	$x = -4$	or	$x = \frac{1}{3}$

These are the three solutions to the original cubic polynomial equation. Check them in the original equation to verify their correctness.

Example of Solving a Quadratic Polynomial by the Grouping Method:

$x^2 + (5b - 2a)x - 10ab = 0$

$x^2 + 5bx - 2ax - 10ab = 0$ Distributive Property

$x \cdot (x + 5b) - 2a \cdot (x + 5b) = 0$ Determine the common factor for each group of two terms.

$(x + 5b)(x - 2a) = 0$ Rewrite in factored form.

Use the zero-product property to solve each linear factor:

	$x + 5b = 0$	or	$x - 2a = 0$
Therefore,	$x = -5b$	or	$x = 2a$

Example of Solving a Rational Equation by Converting to a Common Denominator:

$$\frac{x - 1}{25} = \frac{2}{5}$$

$$\left(\frac{25}{1}\right)\frac{x - 1}{25} = \frac{2}{5}\left(\frac{25}{1}\right)$$

$$\left(\frac{25}{1}\right)\frac{x - 1}{25} = \frac{2}{5}\left(\frac{25}{1}\right) = \frac{2}{1}\left(\frac{5}{1}\right) = 10$$

$$x - 1 = 10$$

Chapter 6: Equations and Problem Solving (cont.)

Example of Solving a Rational Equation:

$$\frac{7}{a} - \frac{1}{3} = \frac{5}{a}$$

$$(3a)\left(\frac{7}{a} - \frac{1}{3}\right) = \frac{5}{a}(3a)$$

$$\frac{3a}{1}\left(\frac{7}{a}\right) - \left(\frac{3a}{1}\right)\left(\frac{1}{3}\right) = \frac{5}{a}\left(\frac{3a}{1}\right)$$

$$\frac{21a}{a} - \frac{3a}{3} = \frac{15a}{a}$$

$$21 - a = 15$$

$$21 - a - 21 = 15 - 21$$

$$-a = -6$$

$$\frac{-a}{-1} = \frac{-6}{-1}$$

$$a = 6$$

Practice: Equations—Linear, Quadratic, Polynomial

Directions: Write the following in general quadratic equation form.

1. $x(3x - 5) = 0$ _____

2. $2x(x + 9)$ _____

3. $-3x(2x - 6)$ _____

4. $3x(5 - x) = 5$ _____

5. $(-a - 5)(a + 6) = 0$ _____

6. $(x - 2)(x - 4) = 0$ _____

7. $(3x - 5)(x + 2) = 0$ _____

Chapter 6: Equations and Problem Solving (cont.)

8. $(-2x + 3)(5x - 1) = 0$ _____

9. $(2x - 3)(5x - 1) = 0$ _____

10. $(x - 9)(x + 2) = 0$ _____

Directions: Use factoring to solve the following quadratic equations. Use your own paper to work the problems.

11. $x^2 - 7x = 0$ _____

12. $2x^2 - 9x = 0$ _____

13. $20x^2 + 60x = 0$ _____

14. $x^2 + 6x + 8 = 0$ _____

15. $x^2 - 7x - 8 = 0$ _____

16. $2x^2 - 5x - 7 = 0$ _____

17. $x^2 - 7x - 44 = 0$ _____

18. $3x^2 - 11x + 6 = 0$ _____

19. $4x^2 + 19x - 5 = 0$ _____

20. $6x^2 = 13x - 6$ _____

21. $x^2 + 5x = 24$ _____

22. $8x^2 - 3 = -5x$ _____

Name: _____ Date: _____

Chapter 6: Equations and Problem Solving (cont.)

Directions: Use the complete the square method to solve the following quadratic equations.

23. $x^2 - 3x + 2 = 0$ _____

24. $x^2 - 16x + 60 = 0$ _____

25. $x^2 - x = 3$ _____

26. $x^2 = 5x + 14$ _____

27. $x^2 - 4x - 2 = 0$ _____

Directions: Use the quadratic formula to solve the following quadratic equations.

28. $2x^2 + 3x - 5 = 0$ _____

29. $x^2 - 11x + 28 = 0$ _____

30. $5x^2 = x + 4$ _____

31. $7x + 6 = 3x^2$ _____

32. $x^2 + 2x - 1 = 0$ _____

33. $2x^2 - 5x = 2$ _____

Directions: Use a quadratic equation to solve the following.

34. Find two consecutive integers whose product is 240. _____

35. The altitude of a triangle is 5 inches less than its base. What are the base and altitude of the triangle if the area of the triangle is 102 square inches? _____

Name: _____ Date: _____

Chapter 6: Equations and Problem Solving (cont.)

(36.) The length of the top of a rectangular desk is 24 inches more than the width. What are the dimensions of the desk if the area of the top is 1,620 square inches?

_____

(37.) A number of coins can be placed in a square array with 14 coins per side. It can also be arranged in a rectangular array with 21 more coins in the length than in the width. How many coins are on the length and width of the rectangular array?

_____

(38.) One square has a side two feet longer than the side of a second square. The area of the larger square is 9 times larger than the area of the smaller square. What is the length of the side of each square?

_____

(39.) The length of a rectangle is 6 inches more than its width. Its area is 40 square inches. What are the dimensions of the rectangle?

_____

Directions: Use the properties of quadratic equations to solve the following cubic equations.

(40.) $6x^3 = 13x^2 - 6x$ _____

(41.) $x^3 = 24x - 5x^2$ _____

(42.) Write in factored form. $6 + 2a + 3b + ab$ _____

Directions: Solve the following rational equations.

(43.) $x = \dfrac{x-2}{x+3} = 2$ _____

(44.) $\dfrac{1}{x-1} = \dfrac{1}{2} + \dfrac{1}{x}$ _____

(45.) $\dfrac{3x}{x+1} + 2x = -4$ _____

Name: _____ Date: _____

Chapter 6: Equations and Problem Solving (cont.)

Challenge Problems: Equations—Linear, Quadratic, Polynomial

1. Use factoring to solve. $3y^2 = \frac{10}{3} - \frac{3}{2}y$ _____

2. Use the complete the square method to solve. $2x^2 = 2 + x$ _____

3. Use the quadratic formula to solve. $2x^2 = 5x - 5$ _____

4. Moki is cutting a rectangular lawn that is 20 feet wide and 80 feet long. If he is cutting a border around the outside, how wide must the border be so that he knows when he has completed half the lawn? _____

5. Solve. $\dfrac{1}{x-2} = \dfrac{1}{x} + \dfrac{1}{3}$

Checking Progress: Equations—Linear, Quadratic, Polynomial

1. Write in general quadratic form. $(2 - x)(5 - 2x)$ _____

2. Use factoring to solve. $x^2 - 2x - 99 = 0$ _____

3. Use factoring to solve. $2x^2 - 15x + 12 = 0$ _____

4. Use the complete the square method to solve. $x^2 + 4x = 96$ _____

5. Use the complete the square method to solve. $x^2 - 5x - 3 = 0$ _____

6. Use the quadratic equation to solve. $x^2 - 3x - 5 = 0$ _____

7. Use the quadratic equation to solve. $2x^2 - 3x - 2 = 0$ _____

8. If 3 is subtracted from 5 times a number, and the result is increased by twice the square of the number, the result is zero. What is the number? _____

9. Solve the equation. $3x^3 - x^2 - 10x = 0$ _____

10. Solve the equation. $\dfrac{5}{x} - 5 = \dfrac{x-1}{x+2}$ _____

Chapter 7: Graphing

Basic Overview: The Cartesian Coordinate System

The **Cartesian coordinate system** is a grid system, like a rectangular map, that is formed by two **axes** (number lines) that are drawn perpendicular to each other. The two intersecting axes (*x*-axis and *y*-axis) form four **quadrants**, illustrated below.

The point of intersection of the two axes is called the **origin**. The horizontal axis is called the *x*-axis and it has increasing positive values to the right of the origin. The vertical axis is called the *y*-axis, and it increases in positive values above the origin. At the origin, the value of both *x* and *y* is equal to zero.

Each point in the grid system is identified by an **ordered pair** of numbers, written as (*x*, *y*). The first number in the ordered pair is called the ***x*-coordinate**, and the second number is called the ***y*-coordinate**. Notice that the origin corresponds to the ordered pair, (0, 0). Locating a point, *P*, that corresponds to an ordered pair (*a*, *b*) in the plane, or grid, is referred to as **plotting** or graphing the point. In general, a **graph** is a set of points in the rectangular coordinate system.

Examples of Graphing With the Cartesian Coordinate System

Example of the Cartesian Coordinate System:

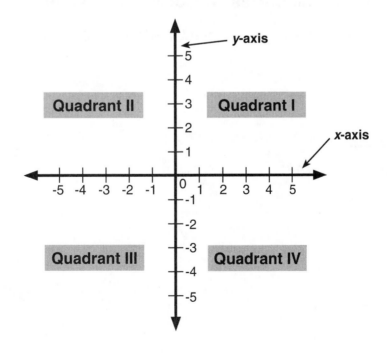

Name: _____ Date: _____

Chapter 7: Graphing (cont.)

Example of Plotting Points Using Ordered Pairs:

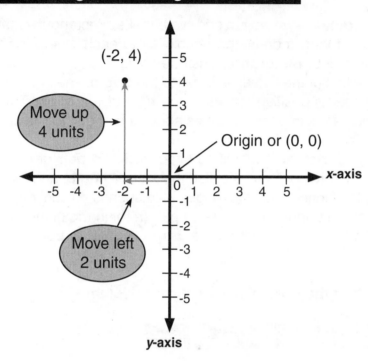

Practice: Graphing With the Cartesian Coordinate System

Directions: In questions 1–7, specify the quadrant in which the point would be located.

1. (2, 3) _____

2. (-5, -6) _____

3. (-51, 6) _____

4. (7, 0) _____

5. (13, -2) _____

6. (-5.2, 6.9021) _____

Chapter 7: Graphing (cont.)

7. $((-5)^2, -6)$ _____

8. If (x, y) is in quadrant II, then in what quadrant is $(x, -y)$? _____

9. If (x, y) is in quadrant II, then in what quadrant is $(-x, y)$? _____

10. What is the point that is 6 units below $(2, 4)$? _____

11. If you are at point $(2, -2)$ and go 6 units to the left and 2 units up, in what quadrant will you be? _____

12. If the point (x, y) is on the y-axis, then what is the value for x? _____

13. Fred started at point $(-51, 6)$. He went to the right 22 units and down 19 units. At what point is he now? _____

14. Frank is now at point $(-5, 6)$. He got there from his starting point by going 9 units to the left and four units up. From where did he start? _____

15. Name three other points with integer coefficients that are on the segment with the endpoints $(4, 9)$ and $(8, 9)$. _____ _____ _____

Challenge Problems: Graphing With the Cartesian Coordinate System

1. In which quadrant is the point $(0, 0)$ located? _____

2. In which quadrant is the point that is 5 units above $(-5, -6)$? _____

3. If (x, y) is in quadrant II, then in what quadrant is (y, x)? _____

Name: _____ Date: _____

Chapter 7: Graphing (cont.)

Checking Progress: Graphing With the Cartesian Coordinate System

1. In what quadrant is the point (-4, -6)? _____

2. If the point (7, y) is not in a quadrant, what is the value of y? _____

3. If the point (x, y) is in quadrant III, where is the point (y, -x)? _____

4. Start at point (2, 3) and go 6 units right, 5 units up, 2 units left, and 9 units down. At what point do you end? _____

5. Consider the line segment with the endpoints (0, 5) and (5, 0). What are other points on this segment that have integer coefficients? _____ _____ _____

Directions: Plot the following points on the grid below.

6. (-1, 3)

7. (6, 7)

8. (4, -5)

9. (-2, -6)

10. (0, 4)

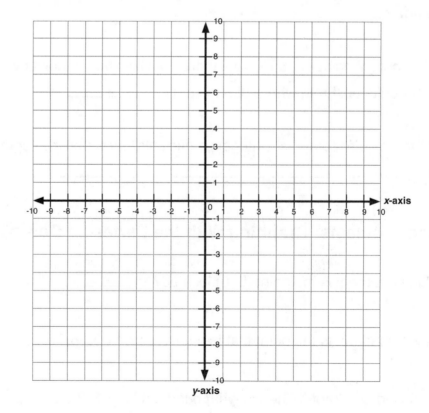

Chapter 8: Functions

Basic Overview: Functions—Tables, Graphs, Notation

A **relation** is defined as any set of ordered pairs, (x, y). The set of all first-coordinate values for the set of ordered pairs in the relation is called the **domain**. The set of all second-coordinate values is called the **range**.

A **function** is a special type of relation in which no two ordered pairs have the same first coordinate and a different second coordinate. That is, each domain value corresponds to exactly one, and only one, range value.

A function can be thought of as a rule that takes an **input** value from the domain and returns an **output** value in the range. We typically choose the input values, so this variable is called the **independent variable** of the function. Since the output values depend on the choice of the input, we call this variable the **dependent variable** of the function.

A function can be indicated by a set of ordered pairs, or by an equation in two variables, or by a graph in the plane. The notation used to describe that "y is a function of x," is $y = f(x)$, which is usually read as "f of x" or "f at x." Notice that since $y = f(x)$, we can also call y the functional value of an ordered pair. Also note that f is just the name of the function. An example from geometry is: the area of a circle (a) is function of the radius (r) according to the following rule: $A(r) = \pi r^2$. Here we have given the name A to the function, and r is the measured input value of the radius, whereas πr^2 is the calculated output value for the area.

Examples of Functions—Tables, Graphs, Notation

Example of a Table That Defines a Function:

x	y
-1	0
5	6
0	1
7	8

Each input value in the x-column is paired with exactly one output value in the y-column.

Name: _____ Date: _____

Chapter 8: Functions (cont.)

Example of a Graph of a Function Using the Previous Table:

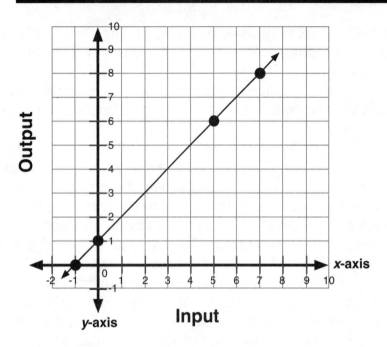

Example of Function Notation:

$f(x) = 2x^2 + x + 1$

What output goes with an input of 3? If $x = 3$, what is $f(3)$?

To find the output value, substitute 3 for x in the rule:

$f(3) = 2(3)^2 + 3 + 1 =$
$2(9) + 3 + 1 =$
$18 + 3 + 1 =$
22

So (3, 22) is an ordered pair that satisfies the rule given for $f(x)$.

Name: _____ Date: _____

Chapter 8: Functions (cont.)

Practice: Functions—Tables, Graphs, Notation

Directions: Decide whether or not the information in the table defines a function, and circle "Yes" or "No."

1. Yes No

x	y
1	3
2	4
3	7
4	19

2. Yes No

x	y
5	3
5	7
2	9
1	11

3. Yes No

x	y
2	6
1	4
1	4
3	7

4. Yes No

x	y
6	1
5	4
4	8
12	0

Chapter 8: Functions (cont.)

Directions: Decide whether or not each set of ordered pairs defines a function, and circle "yes" or "no."

5. Yes   No   (1, 2), (2, 3), (3, 2), (4, 2)

6. Yes   No   (4, 4), (5, 4), (7, 4), (19, 19)

7. Yes   No   (13, 12), (12, 9), (13, 9), (12, 12)

8. Yes   No   (1, 1), (100, 100), (1.23, 1), (0, 0.98)

Let $f(x) = \dfrac{x + 1}{x + 5}$:

9. What is $f(0)$? _____

10. What is $f(100)$? _____

11. What is $f(-2)$? _____

12. For what value of x does $f(x) = \frac{12}{16}$? _____

Let $g(x) = x^2 - 4x - 5$:

13. What is $g(1)$? _____

14. What is $g(7)$? _____

15. What is $g(-6)$?

16. For what values of x does $g(x) = 0$? _____

Let $h(x) = 2x^2 - 11x + 15$:

17. What is $h(0)$? _____

Chapter 8: Functions (cont.)

18. What is $h(-11)$? _____

19. What is $h(2)$? _____

20. For what values of x does $h(x) = 0$? _____

If $k(x) = (x - 3)(3x + 4)$:

21. What is $k(0)$? _____

22. What is $k(-6)$? _____

23. What is $k(13)$? _____

24. For what values of x does $k(x) = 0$? _____

25. For the functions h and k below, what is $h(1) - k(1)$? _____

   Let $h(x) = 2x^2 - 11x + 15$ and if $k(x) = (x - 3)(3x + 4)$

Challenge Problems: Functions—Tables, Graphs, Notation

1. For the function, $f(x) = \dfrac{x + 1}{x + 5}$, what is $f(-5)$? _____

2. If $f(x) = 3x^3 + 11x^2 - 4x$, for what values of x does $f(x) = 0$? _____

3. For the function $h(x) = 2x^2 - 11x + 15$, what is $h(5) - h(4)$? _____

4. For the function $h(x) = 2x^2 - 11x + 15$, what is $h(-x)$? _____

5. For the function $k(x) = (x - 3)(3x + 4)$, what is $k(x + 1)$? _____

Name: _____ Date: _____

Chapter 8: Functions (cont.)

Checking Progress: Functions – Tables, Graphs, Notation

1. Yes   No   Does the information in the table define a function?

x	y
1	13
5	4
3	17
4	19

2. What value of b will make the following table not represent a function? _____

x	y
4	3
5	17
4	b
1	11

3. Yes   No   Do these ordered pairs define a function? (1, 1), (2, 1), (3, 1), (4, 1)

4. What value of b will make the following ordered pairs not represent a function? (3, 4), (4, 5), (5, 6), (6, 7), (4, b) _____

For questions 5–10, use $f(x) = x^2 + 9x - 22$.

5. What is $f(0)$? _____

6. What is $f(-10)$? _____

7. What is $f(5)$? _____

8. For what values of x does $f(x) = 0$? _____

9. What is $f(4) - f(3)$? _____

10. What is $f(x + 2)$? _____

Chapter 9: Linear Functions

Basic Overview: Standard Form, Graphing, Slope, and Writing Equations for a Line

Linear functions all have the same standard form, $f(x) = mx + b$, where m and b can be any real number, including fractions, decimals, integers, or irrational numbers. The reason that functions of the form $f(x) = mx + b$ are called linear functions is because their graphs are straight lines. An important characteristic of a straight line is its steepness, or **slope**. The numerical coefficient, m, of the x term in the standard form is the value of the slope. When two points, (x_1, y_1) and (x_2, y_2), on the line are known, the slope can be found by using the following calculation: $m = \dfrac{y_2 - y_1}{x_2 - x_1}$.

The standard form, $f(x) = mx + b$, is also known as the **slope-intercept form** of a line. This is because the coefficient on the x term, m, is the slope of the line and the value b represents the y-intercept for the graph of the line, the point $(0, b)$.

The Point-Slope Form: Let m be the slope of a line passing through the point (x_1, y_1), then the equation of the line can be written as $y - y_1 = m(x - x_1)$.

The equation of a linear function can be written if (1) the slope and y-intercept are given; (2) the slope and any point are given; or (3) any two points on the line are given.

Examples of Linear Functions in Standard Form; Graphing, Slope, and Writing Equations for a Line

Examples of Linear Functions in Standard Form:

$f(x) = -3x + 5$

$g(x) = \frac{4}{5}x - 2$

$y = 0.35x + 0.78$

$f(x) = 2x + \sqrt{3}$

Chapter 9: Linear Functions (cont.)

Example of Graphing Linear Functions:

$f(x) = -3x + 5$

x	y
-1	-3(-1) + 5 = 8
3	-3(3) + 5 = -4
0	-3(0) + 5 = 5
2	-3(2) + 5 = -1

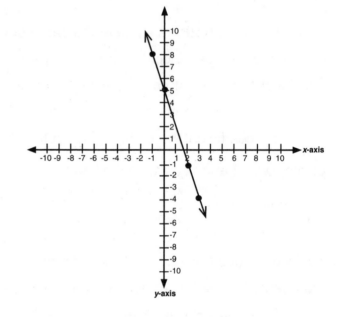

Example of the Slope of a Line:

Two points: (-2, 2) and (4, -1)

The slope of the line will be $-\frac{1}{2}$.

$$\text{slope} = \frac{y_2 - y_1}{x_2 - x_1} = \frac{-1 - 2}{4 - -2} = \frac{-3}{6} = \frac{-1}{2}$$

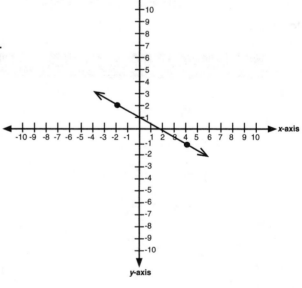

Algebra Practice

Chapter 9: Linear Functions

Chapter 9: Linear Functions (cont.)

Example of Point-Intercept Form:

$y = 3x + 2$

The slope of the line is $m = 3$ and the y-intercept is the point $(0, 2)$.

$$\frac{3}{1} = \frac{rise}{run} = \frac{vertical\ change}{horizontal\ change}$$

Plot the given y-intercept point $(0, 2)$.

From that point, count up 3 units (the vertical change, or rise), and then from that location, move 1 unit to the right (the horizontal change, or run). This locates another point on the line.

With these two points, having determined the graph for the given linear function, connect and draw the arrows.

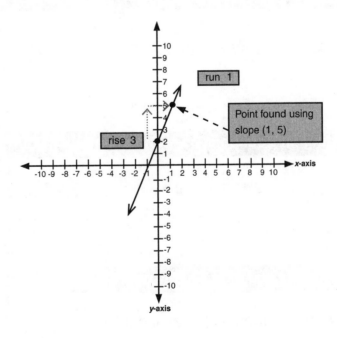

CD-404042 © Mark Twain Media, Inc., Publishers   69

Chapter 9: Linear Functions (cont.)

Examples of Point-Slope Form:

A line with slope $m = \frac{4}{5}$ and passing through the point (4, 11)
The equation for this line is $y - 11 = \frac{4}{5}(x - 4)$.

$y - 11 = \frac{4}{5}(x - 4)$

$y - 11 = \frac{4}{5} \cdot x - \frac{4}{5} \cdot 4$

$y - 11 = \frac{4}{5}x - \frac{16}{5}$

$y - 11 + 11 = \frac{4}{5}x - \frac{16}{5} + 11 =$

$y = \frac{4}{5}x - \frac{16}{5} + \frac{55}{5} =$

$y = \frac{4}{5}x - \frac{39}{5}$

This indicates that the y-intercept is $\left(0, -\frac{39}{5}\right)$ with a slope of $\frac{4}{5}$.

Example of Writing an Equation When Given the Slope and y-intercept:

Let the slope be $m = -5$, and the y-intercept be (0, 3).

$y = mx + b$

$y = -5x + 3$

Example of Writing an Equation Given Slope and Any Point:

Let the slope be $m = 0.75$, and the point be (0.5, 6).

$y - y_1 = m(x - x_1)$

$y - 6 = 0.75(x - 0.5)$

Example of Writing an Equation Given Two Points:

Let the two points given be (3, -2) and (5, 7).

$m = \frac{y_2 - y_1}{x_2 - x_1} = \frac{7 - (-2)}{5 - 3} = \frac{9}{2} = 4.5$

$y - 7 = 4.5(x - 5)$

Name: _____ Date: _____

Chapter 9: Linear Functions (cont.)

Practice: Standard Form, Graphing, Slope, and Writing Equations for a Line

1. For each linear function below, identify the slope and the *y*-intercept.

A. $f(x) = -2x + 5$	slope =	*y*-intercept =
B. $g(x) = 0.45x - 2$	slope =	*y*-intercept =
C. $y = \frac{4}{3}x + \frac{2}{5}$	slope =	*y*-intercept =
D. $5y = 4x + 1$	slope =	*y*-intercept =
E. $h(x) = 5.43x - 8.76$	slope =	*y*-intercept =
F. $g(x) = -\frac{6}{7}x - \frac{4}{5}$	slope =	*y*-intercept =
G. $f(x) = 2.13x - 5.42$	slope =	*y*-intercept =
H. $y = 5.6 - 3.5x$	slope =	*y*-intercept =
I. $4.5x - y = 7$	slope =	*y*-intercept =
J. $2y - 8x = 9$	slope =	*y*-intercept =
K. $h(x) = -5.4 + 9x$	slope =	*y*-intercept =

2. On your own graph paper, graph each of the linear functions below by completing a table and plotting the points on a coordinate plane.

A. $f(x) = -5x - 7$ **F.** $k(x) = -3x - 8$

B. $g(x) = \frac{4}{7}x - 9$ **G.** $l(x) = 5 - \frac{7}{4}x$

C. $h(x) = -3x + 2$ **H.** $m(x) = -\frac{1}{7}x + 9$

D. $i(x) = \frac{1}{5}x - 4$ **I.** $n(x) = 1.5x + 2.4$

E. $j(x) = 10 - \frac{1}{7}x$ **J.** $p(x) = -\frac{2}{3}x + 4$

After graphing your lines, answer the following questions.

K. How would you describe the relationship between the graph of $h(x)$ and $k(x)$?

_____

L. What is the slope of $h(x)$? _____ $k(x)$? _____

Chapter 9: Linear Functions (cont.)

M. How would you describe the relationship between the graph of $m(x)$ and $j(x)$?

_____

N. What is the slope of $m(x)$? _____ $j(x)$? _____

O. How would you describe the relationship between the graph of $g(x)$ and $l(x)$?

_____

P. What is the slope of $g(x)$? _____ $l(x)$? _____

Q. How would you describe the relationship between the graph of $f(x)$ and $i(x)$?

_____

R. What is the slope of $f(x)$? _____ $i(x)$? _____

S. How would you describe the relationship between the graph of $n(x)$ and $p(x)$?

_____

T. What is the slope of $n(x)$? _____ $p(x)$? _____

3. Write the equation for the line that satisfies the given information.

A. slope = -5 and y-intercept = 27 _____

B. slope = $\frac{1}{4}$ and through the point (4, 12) _____

C. through the points (5, 4) and (2, -5) _____

D. through the points (6, 15) and (-6, 7) and put into slope-intercept form

_____

E. slope = -2 and y-intercept = 17 _____

F. slope = 9 and through the point ($-\frac{1}{3}$, 0.4) _____

G. through the points (4.5, 2.3) and (2.5, -4.7) _____

H. through the points ($\frac{7}{2}$, $\frac{4}{5}$) and ($\frac{9}{2}$, $\frac{6}{5}$) and put into slope-intercept form

_____

I. slope = $-\frac{4}{45}$ and y-intercept = $-\frac{123}{456}$ _____

Name: _____ Date: _____

Chapter 9: Linear Functions (cont.)

J. slope = 0.75 and through the point (20, -9) _____

K. through the points (4, 14) and (2, 5)

_____

L. through the points (-15, 12) and (-20, 10) and put into

slope-intercept form _____

4. Tanya and Dave were working for Uncle Berber. They were paid each hour; after each hour they worked, they compared the amount of money each had earned. They determined that there was a relationship between the amount of money they each had earned. They expressed the relationship as $y = 1.5x + 9$, where x, and y, respectively, represent the amount of money Tanya and Dave had at any hour.

A. How much money did Tanya have when Dave had $5? _____

B. How much money did Dave have when Tanya had $21? _____

C. What is the smallest value for y that could occur? _____

D. What is a possible meaning for the 9 in the equation? _____

Challenge Problems: Standard Form, Graphing, Slope, and Writing Equations for a Line

1. Aaron claims that the slope of the line $y = -2x + 15$ is $-\frac{2}{15}$, and Noah disagrees with him and says that the slope is -2. Who is correct and why?

_____

_____

2. Jamie believes that the lines $y = 4x + 3$ and $3x + 12y = 19$ are perpendicular. However, her friend Mike believes that these lines are parallel. With whom do you agree and why?

_____

_____

3. Find the equation of a line in point-slope form that is parallel to $y = 5x - 2$ and goes through the point (9, 1).

_____

Name: _____ Date: _____

Chapter 9: Linear Function (cont.)

Checking Progress: Standard Form, Graphing, Slope, and Writing Equations for a Line

1. For each linear function below, identify the slope and the *y*-intercept.

A. $f(x) = -7x + 2$	slope =	*y*-intercept =
B. $g(x) = -\frac{1}{4}x - \frac{2}{87}$	slope =	*y*-intercept =
C. $y = 0.54x + 0.45$	slope =	*y*-intercept =

2. On your own graph paper, graph each of the linear functions below by completing a table and plotting the points on a coordinate plane.

A. $f(x) = -3x + 2$

B. $g(x) = -\frac{5}{4}x - 1$

C. $h(x) = \frac{1}{3}x + 9$

D. $p(x) = -\frac{5}{4}x + 14$

After graphing your lines, answer the following questions.

E.   How would you describe the relationship between the graph of $f(x)$ and $h(x)$?

_____

F.   What is the slope of $f(x)$? _____ $h(x)$? _____

G.   How would you describe the relationship between the graph of $g(x)$ and $p(x)$?

_____

H.   What is the slope of $g(x)$? _____ $p(x)$? _____

3. Write the equation for the line that satisfies the given information.

A.   slope = $-\frac{3}{2}$ and *y*-intercept = $\frac{15}{16}$ _____

B.   slope = 1.2 and through the point (15, 9) _____

C.   through the points (4, 3) and (-1, 8) _____

D.   through the points (2, 11) and (8, 13) and put into slope-intercept form

_____

Chapter 10: Quadratic Functions

Basic Overview: Standard Form, Graphing Quadratic Functions

A **quadratic function** is any function of the form, $f(x) = ax^2 + bx + c$, where a, b, and c are real numbers and $a \neq 0$. Since the degree of a quadratic function is two, we say that quadratic functions are polynomial functions of degree two.

One approach to graphing a quadratic function is to set up a table of ordered pairs. Choose some input values for x, and compute the related output values for y. Using these ordered pairs from the table, plot them on the coordinate system and then connect the points to form the graph of the function. For example, suppose we want to graph the quadratic function, $f(x) = x^2$. The table below shows one choice of ordered pairs that could be used to sketch the graph of the function. The resulting graph reveals a shape called a **parabola**. It is easy to tell whether the graph of the quadratic function, $f(x) = ax^2 + bx + c$, will be a parabola opening up or opening down. Look at the coefficient a of the ax^2 term of the function rule. If a is positive, the parabola opens up (holding water like a bowl), and if a is negative, the parabola opens down (shedding water like an umbrella).

x	y
-1	1
2	4
0	0
1	1

The **vertex** of the parabola for the graph of a quadratic function of the form, $f(x) = ax^2 + bx + c$, is located at the point $\left(\frac{-b}{2a}, f\left(\frac{-b}{2a}\right)\right)$. Using the coefficients a and b, we can determine the x-coordinate for the vertex, and then evaluate the functional value to obtain the y-coordinate for the vertex. To complete the graph of a quadratic function, it is helpful to locate the x-intercept(s) and the y-intercept of the graph. To locate the y-intercept, set $x = 0$ and find the value of $f(0)$. Notice that this value is always c. That is, $f(0) = c$, for all quadratic functions. Hence, the point $(0, c)$ will be the y-intercept of the graph on the graph of the parabola.

The graph of a quadratic function might not intersect the x-axis at all. It might touch at one point (think of $f(x) = x^2$ touching only at $(0, 0)$), or it might intersect the x-axis at two points. The x-intercept value(s) can be found by using either the factoring method for quadratic equations or the quadratic formula. Set the given quadratic function equal to zero, that is, $ax^2 + bx + c = 0$ and solve for x.

Chapter 10: Quadratic Functions (cont.)

Examples of Quadratic Functions

Examples of Quadratic Functions in Standard Form:

$$f(x) = x^2 + 3x + 4$$

$$g(t) = -2t^2 + 7$$

$$h(x) = \tfrac{2}{3}x^2 + 6x$$

Examples of Graphing Quadratic Functions:

The graph of $g(x) = -x^2$ is the mirror image of $f(x) = x^2$. It is the same parabola, but it opens down rather than opening up as is seen in the figures below.

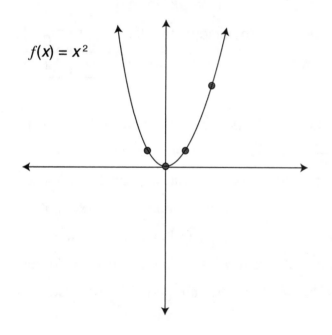

$f(x) = x^2$

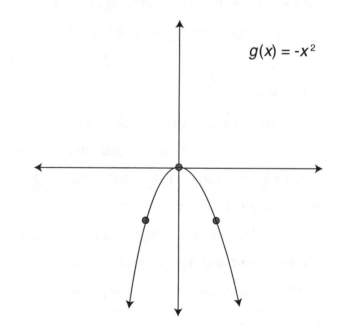

$g(x) = -x^2$

Chapter 10: Quadratic Functions (cont.)

Example of the Vertex of the Parabola Defined by the Quadratic Function of the Form:

Consider the quadratic function, $f(x) = -2x^2 + 6x + 1$. Find the vertex.

Note: $a = -2$ and $b = 6$

The x-coordinate is $\dfrac{-b}{2a} = \dfrac{-6}{2(-2)} = \dfrac{-6}{-4} = \dfrac{3}{2} = 1.5$

The y-coordinate is $f(1.5) = -2(1.5)^2 + 6(1.5) + 1 = 5.5$

The vertex for the parabola will be at the point (1.5, 5.5).

Note: the parabola will open down from this point since the coefficient on x^2 is -2.

Example of Finding the x- and y-intercepts:

$f(x) = x^2 + x - 12$

Find the y-intercept:

Let $x = 0$, find $f(0) = 0^2 + 0 - 12 = -12$, so the point (0, -12) is the y-intercept.

Find the x-intercept: Let $y = f(x) = 0$ and solve for x.

$0 = x^2 + x - 12$ Try factoring as the first method of solution.

$0 = (x - 3)(x + 4)$

$0 = x - 3$ or $0 = x + 4$

$x = 3$ or $x = -4$

This means that the parabola will intersect the x-axis in two points (3, 0) and (-4, 0).

The vertex for this parabola is $x = -\frac{1}{2}$ (by substitution in $x = \dfrac{-b}{2a}$)

And $f(-\frac{1}{2}) = (-\frac{1}{2})^2 + (-\frac{1}{2}) - 12 = -\frac{49}{4}$,

so the vertex point is $(-\frac{1}{2}, -\frac{49}{4})$.

The parabola opens up because the coefficient on x^2 is positive.

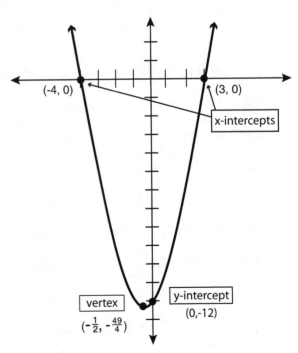

Name: _____ Date: _____

Chapter 10: Quadratic Functions (cont.)

Practice: Quadratic Functions

1. Complete the table below:

Function	Parabola Opens Up or Down	*y*-intercept
A. $f(x) = 3x^2$		
B. $g(x) = -\frac{1}{2}x^2 - 2x + 1$		
C. $h(x) = 4x^2 + 10x$		
D. $f(x) = 0.23x^2 - 0.5x + 1$		
E. $g(x) = \frac{1}{5}x^2 + 5$		
F. $h(x) = -0.45x^2 - 0.24x + 0.1$		
G. $f(x) = 2x^2 + 7$		
H. $g(x) = \frac{3}{7}x^2 - \frac{4}{5}x + \frac{1}{3}$		
I. $h(x) = -\frac{5}{9}x^2$		
J. $f(x) = 0.75x^2 - 3x + \frac{2}{9}$		
K. $g(x) = -12x^2 + 21$		

2. For each quadratic function below, find the vertex of the parabola.

A. $y = x^2 - 2x + 8$ _____

B. $y = 3x^2 + x - 6$ _____

C. $y = 5x^2$ _____

D. $y = -0.2x^2 + 0.5$ _____

E. $y = -4x^2 + 3x + 9$ _____

F. $y = x^2 - 2x$ _____

G. $y = -5x^2 + 2x + 3$ _____

H. $y = x^2 + \frac{3}{4}x - 6$ _____

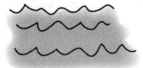

Name: _____ Date: _____

Chapter 10: Quadratic Functions (cont.)

(I.) $y = -\frac{1}{2}x^2 - 0.75x - 4$

(J.) $y = -2x^2 - 0.2x + \frac{1}{2}$ _____

(K.) $y = 3x^2 + \frac{8}{3}$ _____

3.) For each quadratic function, find the *x*-intercepts, if they exist.

(A.) $y = x^2 - 2x + 8$ _____

(B.) $y = 3x^2 + x - 6$ _____

(C.) $y = 5x^2$ _____

(D.) $y = -0.2x^2 + 0.5$ _____

(E.) $y = 70x^2 + 99x - 36$ _____

(F.) $y = x^2 - 2x$ _____

(G.) $y = -12x^2 - 17x + 40$ _____

(H.) $y = x^2 + \frac{3}{4}x - 6$ _____

(I.) $y = 0.1x^2 - x - 20$ _____

(J.) $y = -2x^2 - 0.2x + \frac{1}{2}$ _____

(K.) $y = \frac{3}{8}x^2 - \frac{1}{12}x - \frac{2}{9}$ _____

4.) On your own paper, graph the function given by $y = 3x^2 + 4$.

5.) On your own paper, graph the function given by $y = -x^2 - 3x + 7$.

6.) On your own paper, graph the function given by $y = 0.5x^2 + 2x - 8$.

7.) On your own paper, graph the function given by $y = -4x^2 - 3x$.

Name: _____ Date: _____

Chapter 10: Quadratic Functions (cont.)

Challenge Problems: Quadratic Functions

1.) Yanta needs help to determine by looking at a quadratic equation whether it opens up or down and is wide or narrow. What should Yanta look at in the equation to help her? How can you tell if a parabola opens up? How can you tell if a parabola will be narrow?

_____

_____

_____

_____

2.) Katie said that she found the vertex for the parabola $2x^2 + 5x - 3$ to be $(-\frac{5}{4}, -\frac{49}{8})$, and Arthur said that he found the vertex to be $(-\frac{5}{4}, -\frac{99}{8})$. Who is correct and why?

_____

_____

_____

3.) Neelie says that she can tell quickly that a parabola has no x-intercepts by using part of the quadratic formula. She knows that $3x^2 - 5x + 8$ has no x-intercepts without trying to find them. Verify or disprove Neelie's claim.

_____

_____

_____

_____

4.) Explain in written words what the graph of $6x^2 + 7.3x + 2$ looks like. Make sure to mention the vertex, x-intercepts, the direction in which the parabola opens, and whether it is narrow or wide.

_____

_____

_____

_____

Name: _____ Date: _____

Chapter 10: Quadratic Functions (cont.)

Checking Progress: Quadratic Functions

1.) Complete the table:

Function	Parabola Opens Up or Down	Narrow or Wide
A. $f(x) = -x^2 - 5$		
B. $g(x) = 1.75x^2 - 3x + 4$		
C. $h(x) = -\frac{1}{4}x^2 + 23x$		

2.) For each quadratic function below, find the vertex for the parabola.

A. $y = -3x^2 - 5x + 2$ _____

B. $y = 0.55x^2 + 0.32x - 6.4$ _____

C. $y = \frac{1}{12}x^2 - \frac{2}{9}x + \frac{5}{13}$ _____

3.) For each quadratic function, find the *x*-intercepts, if they exist.

A. $y = 45x^2 - 43x + 10$ _____

B. $y = 0.45x - \frac{1}{5}x + 12$ _____

C. $y = x^2 + x - 42$ _____

4.) On your own paper, graph the function given by $y = x^2 + x - 6$.

Name: _____   Date: _____

Check-Up Problems: Number Systems

Directions: Using the words listed below, fill in the blanks with the correct number type(s).

Real Number	**Rational Number**	**Integer**
Whole Number	**Irrational Number**	

Number	**Type or Types**
1. $-3.212212\overline{212}$	_____
2. $\sqrt{5}$	_____
3. $\sqrt{441}$	_____
4. $\frac{46}{23}$	_____
5. $\sqrt{\pi^2}$	_____
6. $0.341341\overline{341}$	_____
7. 0.134^2	_____
8. $\sqrt{13^2}$	_____
9. $-134,134,134,134$	_____
10. $\frac{\pi}{0}$	_____

Name: _____ Date: _____

Check-Up Problems: Properties

Directions: In questions 1–5, use one of the properties of real numbers to generate a solution to the problem.

1. $312 + (-5,666) + 1,082 + (-312) + 512 + (-1,082) + 5,666 =$ _____

2. _____ $+ (29 \cdot 6) = (29 \cdot 6) + 253$

3. $13a + (19b \cdot 4z) = ($ _____ $\cdot 4z) + 13a$

4. $39a + ($ _____ $+$ _____ $) = (39a + 49z) + 32a$

5. Use the Associative Property to mentally compute the following. $(872 + 961) + 39$

   _____

6. Explain how to mentally compute the following by using the Associative Property of Multiplication. $(792,234 \cdot 50) \cdot 2$

   _____

   _____

7. Use the Distributive Property to mentally simplify. $(13 \cdot 25) + (13 \cdot 5).$ _____

8. Use reciprocals to mentally compute. $\frac{3}{7} \cdot 15 \cdot \frac{7}{3}.$ _____

9. Rewrite using the Distributive Property. $431c^5 + 29c^2$ _____

10. Which property is illustrated? $(12 \cdot 71) + 13 = (71 \cdot 12) + 13$ _____

Name: _____ Date: _____

Check-Up Problems: Exponents and Exponential Expressions

Directions: Complete the following problems.

1. Evaluate. 0.2^5 _____

2. Evaluate. -3^3 _____

3. What is the largest integer value for b so that $b^3 < 10,000$? _____

4. Evaluate. $8^2 \cdot 10^2$ _____

5. Evaluate. $(-2 \cdot -5)^3$ _____

6. Combine terms. $4a^2 - 3b^4 - 7a^2 - 4b^4$ _____

7. Combine terms. $4a^2 - [3b^4 - (7a^2 - 4b^4)]$ _____

8. Combine terms. $(a^4)^2 \cdot b^{91} \cdot (b^7)^5 \cdot a^{41} \cdot b^2$ _____

9. Rewrite using only positive exponents. -2^{-4} _____

10. Combine terms. $[(y^7)^5]^{12}$ _____

Name: _____ Date: _____

Check-Up Problems: Roots and Radical Expressions

Directions: Complete the following problems.

1. $\sqrt{(225)(49)}$ _____

2. $\sqrt{961}$ _____

3. $\sqrt{144z^{24}}$ _____

4. $az\sqrt{a^3z^7} \cdot a^2z^2\sqrt{z^3a^7}$, $a > 0$, $z > 0$ _____

5. $\sqrt{(2^{15})(7^4)(13^3)}$ _____

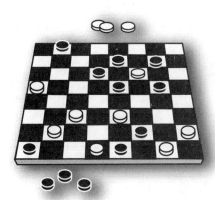

6. $\sqrt{66} \cdot \sqrt{55}$ _____

7. $\dfrac{\sqrt{143}}{\sqrt{88}}$ _____

8. $\left(\dfrac{\sqrt{18}}{\sqrt{24}}\right)\left(\dfrac{\sqrt{30}}{\sqrt{80}}\right)$ _____

9. $11\sqrt{12z} - 2\sqrt{75z}$ _____

10. $15\sqrt{20z^9} - 14\sqrt{45z^3}$ _____

Name: _____ Date: _____

Check-Up Problems: Operations on Algebraic Expressions

Directions: Complete the following problems.

1. $31a + 9y + 1.7y$ _____

2. $3.2x - 0.19x + 0.17y$ _____

3. $\frac{5}{2}\left(x - \frac{21}{2}x\right)$ _____

4. $3.1xz^3 \cdot 0.03x^2z$ _____

5. $0.1x^5y^2z^3 \div 0.25x^2yz$ _____

6. $\dfrac{98x^4yz^3w}{18xz^5yw^2}$ _____

7. $|12| - [-|(4 \cdot (3 - 6)|]$ _____

8. $\frac{14}{12} \cdot \frac{15}{21} \cdot \frac{3}{5}$ _____

9. $\frac{1}{5} + \frac{2}{7} + \frac{3}{11}$ _____

10. $11x - (3x - \{- [8 \cdot (-5x + 2x)] - 17x\})$ _____

Name: _____ Date: _____

Check-Up Problems: Equations and Problem Solving

Directions: Complete the following problems. Use your own paper if you need more room to work the problems.

1. Write in general quadratic form. $(2 - 3x)(1 + 2x)$ _____

2. Use factoring to solve. $2x^2 + 9x = 35$ _____

3. Use factoring to solve. $x^2 + 8x - 33 = 0$ _____

4. Use the completing the square method to solve. $x^2 - 6x + 5 = 0$ _____

5. Use the completing the square method to solve. $2x^2 = 12 - 5x$ _____

6. Use the quadratic equation to solve. $x^2 - 3x - 18 = 0$ _____

7. Use the quadratic equation to solve. $3x^2 - x = 2$ _____

8. The width of a rectangle is 5 centimeters less than its length. The area of the rectangle is 374 square centimeters. What are the dimensions of the rectangle? _____

9. Write in factored form. $2ab + 5b - 4a - 10$

   _____

10. Solve the equation. $x + \dfrac{3x}{x - 2} + 1 = 0$

   _____

Name: _____ Date: _____

Check-Up Problems: Graphing

Directions: Answer the following questions.

1. In what quadrant is the point (4, -6.45464646)?

    _____

2. If the point (7, 3*y*) is not in a quadrant, what is the value of *y*?

    _____

3. If the point (*x*, *y*) is in quadrant III, where is the point (-*y*, *x*)?

    _____

4. Start at point (-2, 3) and go 16 units right, 9 units up, 12 units left, and 10 units down. At what point do you end? _____

5. Consider the line segment with endpoints (0, -5) and (5, 0). What are other points on this segment that have integer coefficients? _____

Directions: Plot the following points on the grid.

6. (-9, 2)

7. (4, -5)

8. (0, 7)

9. (-8, -3)

10. (6, -4)

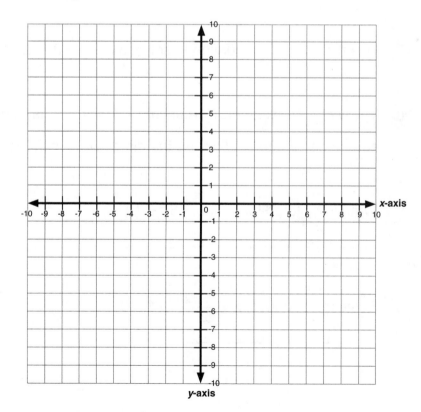

Name: _____ Date: _____

Check-Up Problems: Functions

Directions: Complete the following problems.

1. Does the information in the table below define a function? _____

x	y
1	3
6	14
3	17
1	5

2. What value of *b* will make the following table represent a function? _____

x	y
4	3
5	17
4	b
1	11

3. Do these ordered pairs define a function? (1, 1), (1, 2), (1, 3), (1, 4)

_____

4. What value of *b* will make the following table represent a function? _____

x	y
3	4
4	5
5	6
6	7
4	b

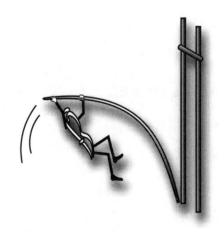

Name: _____ Date: _____

Check-Up Problems: Functions (cont.)

Directions: For questions 5–10, use $f(x) = x^2 - 9x + 8$

5. What is $f(0)$? _____

6. What is $f(10)$? _____

7. What is $f(5)$? _____

8. For what values of x does $f(x) = 0$? _____

9. What is $f(4) - f(3)$? _____

10. What is $f(x + 2)$? _____

Name: _____ Date: _____

Check-Up Problems: Linear Functions

Directions: Complete the following problems.

1. For each linear function below, identify the slope and the *y*-intercept.

A. $f(x) = -12x - \frac{31}{5}$	slope =	*y*-intercept =
B. $g(x) = -2.35x - 3.46$	slope =	*y*-intercept =
C. $y = \frac{1}{3}x + 18$	slope =	*y*-intercept =

2. On your own graph paper, graph each of the linear functions below by completing a table and plotting the points on a coordinate plane.

   A. $f(x) = -2.2x - 4$
   B. $g(x) = \frac{2}{3}x + 8$
   C. $h(x) = \frac{5}{11}x - 1$
   D. $p(x) = \frac{2}{3}x - 3$

After graphing your lines, answer the following on your own paper.

   E. How would you describe the relationship between the graph of $f(x)$ and $h(x)$?
   F. What is the slope of $f(x)$? $h(x)$?
   G. How would you describe the relationship between the graph of $g(x)$ and $p(x)$?
   H. What is the slope of $g(x)$? $p(x)$?

3. Write the equation for the line that satisfies the given information.
   A. slope = $-\frac{5}{12}$ and the *y*-intercept = $\frac{14}{13}$ _____
   B. slope = -3 and through the point (2, -8) _____
   C. through the points (-2, -2) and (4, -5) _____
   D. through the points (-9, -3) and (-4, -8) and put into slope-intercept form

   _____

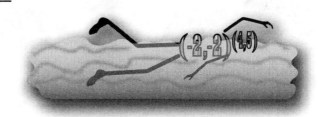

Name: _____ Date: _____

Check-Up Problems: Quadratic Functions

Directions: Complete the following problems.

1. Complete the table.

Function	Parabola Opens Up or Down	Narrow or Wide
A. $f(x) = 2x^2 - 3$		
B. $g(x) = -3.2x^2 + 23.45x$		
C. $h(x) = \frac{2}{3}x^2 - \frac{5}{67}x + 2.1$		

2. For each quadratic function below, find the vertex for the parabola.

    A. $y = 12.3x^2 - 23.4x + 34.5$ _____

    B. $y = \frac{4}{3}x^2 - \frac{2}{5}x + \frac{6}{7}$ _____

    C. $y = -3x^2 - 5x + 34$ _____

3. For each quadratic function, find the *x*-intercepts, if they exist.

    A. $y = 48x^2 + 170x + 143$ _____

    B. $y = -3.4x^2 + 6.7x - 9.1$ _____

    C. $y = \frac{9}{5}x^2 - \frac{26}{5}x + \frac{32}{9}$ _____

4. On your own graph paper, graph the function given by $y = x^2 + 10x + 25$.

Practice Answer Keys

Practice: Number Systems (p. 8–9)

1. rational, real
2. rational, real
3. irrational, real
4. rational, real
5. rational, real
6. integer, rational, real
7. rational, real
8. irrational, real
9. whole, integer, rational, real
10. irrational, real
11. irrational, real
12. rational, real
13. irrational, real
14. whole, integer, rational, real
15. whole, integer, rational, real

Challenge Problems: Number Systems (p. 9)

Answers to these questions can vary. Provided below are examples that answer each question as posed.

1. Let $a = 14$ and $b = 7$
2. Let $a = 12$ and $b = 0$
3. Let $a = \sqrt{3}$ and $b = 2$
4. Let $a = 0$ and $b = 12$
5. Let $a = 4$ and $b = 7$

Checking Progress: Number Systems (p. 10)

1. rational, real
2. whole, integer, rational, real
3. irrational, real
4. rational, real
5. rational, real
6. whole, integer, rational, real
7. irrational, real
8. rational, real
9. irrational, real
10. none

Practice Answer Keys (cont.)

Practice: Properties of Numbers (p. 14–15)
1. Identity Property of Addition
2. Commutative Property of Multiplication
3. Associative Property of Addition
4. Distributive Property of Multiplication Over Addition
5. Identity Property of Multiplication
6. Commutative Property of Multiplication
7. Associative Property of Multiplication
8. Commutative Property of Addition
9. Additive Inverse
10. Commutative Property of Multiplication
11. Multiplicative Inverse
12. $\frac{3}{2}$
13. False
14. True
15. False

Challenge Problems: Properties of Numbers (p. 15)
1. True
2. False
3. False
4. True
5. False

Checking Progress: Properties of Numbers (p. 16)
1. Compute as $(17 + 3) = 20$; $20 + 8 = 28$
2. Compute as $2 \cdot 5 = 10$; $17 \cdot 10 = 170$
3. Compute as $4 + 6 = 10$; $17 \cdot 10 = 170$
4. Compute as $\frac{4}{5} \cdot \frac{5}{4} = 1$; $1 \cdot 81 = 81$
5. 221
6. $21b$
7. $29z + 43a$
8. $3b + 4c$
9. $b^5(513b^3 + 29)$
10. Compute as $8{,}619 + 81 = 8{,}700$; $8{,}700 + 287 = 8{,}987$

Practice: Exponents and Exponential Expressions (p. 17–18)
1. 125
2. 4.41
3. 20
4. 100

Practice Answer Keys (cont.)

5. $4b^2$
6. -243
7. 1,024
8. 2^{13}
9. 4
10. 0
11. False. The expression $(-5)^4$ has a value of 625, while the expression -5^4 has a value of -625.
12. True
13. 100
14. -640
15. 4,000
16. False
17. True
18. True
19. 0.00001
20. 1.024

Challenge Problems: Exponents and Exponential Expressions (p. 18)
1. None
2. 2
3. 3
4. $60x^2y^3$
5. 0.00108

Practice: Combining Terms (p. 20–21)
1. $8x^3$
2. 5^7
3. $2x^2$
4. 2^5
5. $-6x^2$
6. Cannot combine into one term, but could rewrite as $8z(z-1)$.
7. $12z^3 - z$
8. $2^{11}x^8$
9. $-90x^2$
10. $-36x^2$
11. $71x^2$
12. 5
13. 12^{44}
14. $8a + 12b$
15. $12z$

Practice Answer Keys (cont.)

16. $(4^9)(7^3)$
17. Brianna is not correct. She can't combine into one term, only rewrite as $z^3(2 + 3z^2)$
18. $-6z^5$
19. z^{19}
20. z^9

Challenge Problems: Combining Terms (p. 21)

1. $34x$
2. This is not correct, $8z^3 + 8z^3 = 16z^3$
3. This is not correct, $48^5 \div 48^4 = 48^1$, or 48
4. $-15x^5$
5. Judd is correct.

Practice: Raising to a Power and Negative Exponents (p. 23–24)

1. 7^{10}
2. 7^{10}
3. x^{30}
4. $\dfrac{1}{3^4}$
5. $\dfrac{1}{3^8}$
6. 3^8
7. 1
8. $\dfrac{1}{3^4}$
9. $\dfrac{1}{2^5}$
10. 3^4
11. 3^{12}
12. $\dfrac{1}{9^2}$
13. False
14. $x = 1$
15. $x = 0$

Challenge Problems: Raising to a Power and Negative Exponents (p. 24)

1. True
2. No, as $a^{-2} = \dfrac{1}{a^2}$, so it is never a negative number, provided that a is a real number.
3. False
4. Possible answers include: $1, \frac{1}{2}, \frac{1}{3}, \frac{1}{4}$, etc.
5. Frank is right—a larger exponent does not always guarantee a larger number.

Practice Answer Keys (cont.)

Checking Progress: Raising to a Power and Negative Exponents (p. 25)

1. 0.000008
2. -64
3. 5
4. 1,728,000
5. -144
6. $48a^2 - 37b^4$
7. $48a^2 + 31b^4$
8. $a^{17} \cdot b^{34}$
9. $\dfrac{1}{(-2)^2} = \dfrac{1}{4} = 0.25$
10. y^{210}

Practice: Square, Cube and Higher Roots and Negative Radicands (p. 27–28)

1. $2\sqrt[3]{2}$
2. 5
3. 1
4. $3\sqrt[5]{3}$
5. $2\sqrt[4]{3}$
6. $(4^3)\sqrt[3]{4^2}$
7. Not possible
8. -3
9. -1
10. Not possible
11. -3
12. $\dfrac{-3}{5}$ or $-\dfrac{3}{5}$ or $\dfrac{3}{-5}$

Challenge Problems: Square, Cube, and Higher Roots and Negative Radicands (p. 28)

1. Neither. These two expressions both equal 1.
2. Helene is correct.
3. True

Practice 1: Simplifying Radical Expressions (p. 32–33)

1. 4
2. 40
3. 20
4. y^4
5. y^3

Practice Answer Keys (cont.)

6. 10
7. $\sqrt{15}$
8. 76
9. $y^4\sqrt{y}$
10. $4\sqrt{3}$
11. 60
12. 108
13. $\frac{6}{7}$
14. $\frac{2}{3}\sqrt{39}$
15. $\frac{1}{100}\sqrt{10}$
16. 0.1
17. 12
18. $3\sqrt{3}$
19. 75
20. $15\sqrt{15}$

Practice 2: Simplifying Radical Expressions (p. 34)

1. $14\sqrt{3}$
2. $(9x + y)\sqrt{5}$
3. $9x^2\sqrt{x}$
4. $50\sqrt{x} - 17x^2$
5. $10\sqrt{3}$
6. No, it should be $11x^2$.
7. No, $\sqrt{75} = 5\sqrt{3}$
8. $5\sqrt{2y}$
9. $10\sqrt{5} - 6\sqrt{3}$
10. $15y^2$
11. $12\sqrt{3}$
12. Cannot be combined

Practice Answer Keys (cont.)

Challenge Problems 1: Simplifying Radicals (p. 35)

1. $7\sqrt{3}$
2. There is no real number a such that $a^2 = -9$.
3. $a = \frac{5}{3}$
4. True
5. True

Challenge Problems 2: Simplifying Radicals (p. 35)

1. Yes, this is correct.
2. No. It is $14\sqrt{3}$.
3. No.

Practice: Fractional Exponents and Radical Expressions (p. 36–37)

1. $5^{\frac{3}{5}}$
2. $5^{\frac{7}{3}}$
3. $13^{\frac{1}{2}}$
4. $a^{\frac{3}{4}}$
5. $a^{\frac{5}{9}}$
6. $5^{\frac{7}{8}}$
7. $\sqrt{7}$
8. $\sqrt{13y}$
9. $\sqrt{4} = 2$
10. $\sqrt[3]{10^2} = \sqrt[3]{100}$
11. $3 \cdot 5^{\frac{1}{2}}$
12. $\sqrt[3]{17^2}$

Challenge Problems: Fractional Exponents and Radical Expressions (p. 37)

1. False
2. Diane
3. 4 and 5

Checking Progress: Roots and Radical Expressions (p. 38)

1. 63
2. $21\sqrt{2}$
3. $13z^4$
4. $a^2z^3\sqrt{z}$
5. $2^2 \cdot 5^2 \cdot 11^3 \sqrt{2 \cdot 5 \cdot 11} = 133,100\sqrt{110}$

Practice Answer Keys (cont.)

6. $21\sqrt{2}$
7. $\frac{1}{5}\sqrt{55}$
8. $\frac{1}{3}\sqrt{3}$
9. $-z\sqrt{2z}$
10. $(3z^2 + 25z)\sqrt{6z}$

Practice: Operations on Algebraic Expressions (p. 40–43)

1. 65

2. -248

3. Cannot be combined

4. $3(a + 3b + 6c)$

5. $9.8x$

6. $72ab$

7. $\frac{12}{8}$ or $1\frac{1}{2}$

8. $50x - 17a$

9. 21

10. $85a^2$

11. $12(a + b - c)$

12. $7\frac{3}{4}x$

13. $4x(1 - 3y)$

14. $-3\frac{1}{4}$

15. $56x^2yz$

16. $25y(4y + x)$

17. $7x - 3y$

18. $8\frac{1}{4}$

19. $\frac{7y}{2w}$

20. $\frac{10z}{y}$

21. -13

22. 4

Practice Answer Keys (cont.)

23. 8
24. -16
25. 60
26. -15
27. -2
28. 1
29. -1
30. 210
31. 8.72
32. 2.68
33. 3.2
34. -98
35. Division by zero is undefined.
36. 42
37. $\frac{5}{8}$
38. $11x$
39. $\frac{41}{35}$
40. 1.773

Challenge Problems: Operations on Algebraic Expressions (p. 43)
1. Both are correct.
2. $5^9 = 1,953,125$
3. 0
4. 4
5. $49x$

Checking Progress: Operations on Algebraic Expressions (p. 44)
1. Cannot be combined
2. $4.9x - 17y$
3. $-2\frac{3}{4}x$
4. $5.67x^3yz^2$
5. $\dfrac{40yz}{x^2}$
6. $\dfrac{8yz}{3xw}$
7. 0
8. $\frac{5}{8}$

Practice Answer Keys (cont.)

9. $\frac{1}{35}$

10. $15x$

Practice: Equations—Linear, Quadratic, and Polynomial (p. 52–55)

1. $3x^2 - 5x = 0$
2. $2x^2 + 18x - 4 = 0$
3. $-6x^2 + 18x + 1 = 0$
4. $3x^2 - 15x + 5 = 0$ or $-3x^2 + 15x - 5 = 0$
5. $a^2 + 11a + 30 = 0$ or $-a^2 - 11a - 30 = 0$
6. $x^2 - 6x + 5 = 0$
7. $3x^2 + x - 10 = 0$
8. $-10x^2 + 17x - 3 = 0$ or $10x^2 - 17x + 3 = 0$
9. $10x^2 - 17x + 3 = 0$
10. $x^2 - 7x - 18 = 0$
11. $x = 0$ or $x = 7$
12. $x = 0$ or $x = 4.5$
13. $x = 0$ or $x = -3$
14. $x = -4$ or $x = -2$
15. $x = 8$ or $x = -1$
16. $x = -1$ or $x = 3.5$
17. $x = 11$ or $x = -4$
18. $x = 3$ or $x = \frac{2}{3}$
19. $x = -5$ or $x = \frac{1}{4}$
20. $x = \frac{2}{3}$ or $x = \frac{3}{2}$
21. $x = -8$ or $x = 3$
22. $x = -1$ or $x = \frac{3}{8}$
23. $x = 2$ or $x = 1$
24. $x = 10$ or $x = 6$
25. $x = \dfrac{1 + \sqrt{13}}{2}$ or $x = \dfrac{1 - \sqrt{13}}{2}$
26. $x = 7$ or $x = -2$
27. $x = 2 + \sqrt{6}$ or $x = 2 - \sqrt{6}$
28. $x = 1$ or $x = -\frac{5}{2}$
29. $x = 4$ or $x = 7$
30. $x = 1$ or $x = -\frac{4}{5}$
31. $x = 3$ or $x = -\frac{2}{3}$
32. $x = -1 + \sqrt{2}$ or $x = -1 - \sqrt{2}$

Practice Answer Keys (cont.)

33. $x = \dfrac{5 + \sqrt{41}}{4}$ or $x = \dfrac{5 - \sqrt{41}}{4}$

34. If x is the smaller number an equation to use is $x(x + 1) = 240$; 15 and 16

35. If x is the length of the base of the triangle, an equation to use is $\left(\frac{1}{2}\right)x(x - 5) = 102$. The length of the base is 17 inches and length of the altitude is 12 inches.

36. If x is the width of the top, an equation to use is $x(x + 5) = 1{,}620$. The width is 30 inches and length is 54 inches.

37. The array is 7 coins wide and 28 coins long.

38. The length of a side on the small square is 1 foot, and the length of a side of the large square is 3 feet.

39. The width is 4, and the length is 10.

40. $x = 0$, $x = \frac{2}{3}$, or $x = \frac{3}{2}$

41. $x = 0$, $x = -8$, or $x = 3$

42. $(3 + a)(2 + b)$

43. $x = 2$ or $x = -2$

44. $x = 2$ or $x = -1$

45. $x = -0.5$ or $x = -4$

Challenge Problems: Equations—Linear, Quadratic, Polynomial (p. 56)

1. $x = \dfrac{-4}{3}$ or $x = \dfrac{5}{6}$

2. $x = -2 + \sqrt{6}$ or $x = -2 - \sqrt{6}$

3. There are no real roots to this equation.

4. If x is the dimension of the width of the border, then an equation to use is $(20 - 2x)(80 - 2x) = \frac{1}{2} \cdot 20 \cdot 80$. The width is $x = 25 - 5\sqrt{17}$, or approximately 4.38 inches.

5. $x = 1 + \sqrt{7}$ or $x = 1 - \sqrt{7}$

Checking Progress: Equations—Linear, Quadratic, Polynomial (p. 56)

1. $2x^2 - 9x + 10 = 0$

2. $x = 11$ or $x = -9$

3. $x = 1.5$ or $x = 4$

4. $x = 8$ or $x = -12$

5. $x = \dfrac{5 + \sqrt{37}}{2}$ or $x = \dfrac{5 - \sqrt{37}}{2}$

6. $x = \dfrac{3 + \sqrt{29}}{2}$ or $x = \dfrac{3 - \sqrt{29}}{2}$

Practice Answer Keys (cont.)

7. $x = 2$ or $x = -0.5$
8. $x = 0.5$ or $x = -3$
9. $x = 0$ or $x = 2$ or $x = -(\frac{5}{3})$
10. $x = 1$ or $x = -(\frac{5}{3})$

Practice: Graphing With the Cartesian Coordinate System (p. 58–59)
1. I
2. III
3. II
4. It is not located in any quadrant.
5. IV
6. II
7. IV
8. III
9. I
10. (2, -2)
11. You will not be in a quadrant, you will be on the x-axis.
12. $x = 0$
13. (-29, -13)
14. (4, 2)
15. (5, 9), (6, 9), and (7, 9)

Challenge Problems: Graphing With the Cartesian Coordinate System (p. 59)
1. It is not located in any quadrant.
2. The new point would be (-5, -1) and is in quadrant III.
3. IV

Checking Progress: Graphing With the Cartesian Coordinate System (p. 60)
1. III
2. $y = 0$
3. II
4. (6, -1)
5. (1, 4), (2, 3), (3, 2), and (4, 1)
6–10. See grid at right.

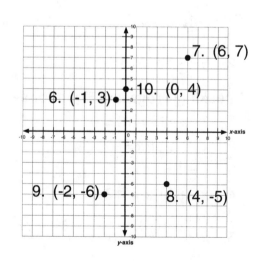

Practice Answer Keys (cont.)

Practice: Functions—Tables, Graphs, Notation (p. 63–65)

1. Yes
2. No
3. Yes
4. Yes
5. Yes
6. Yes
7. No
8. Yes
9. $\frac{1}{5}$
10. $\frac{101}{105}$
11. $-\left(\frac{1}{3}\right)$
12. 11
13. -8
14. 16
15. 55
16. $x = 5$ or $x = -1$
17. 15
18. 378
19. 1
20. $x = 2.5$ or $x = 3$
21. -12
22. 126
23. 430
24. $x = 3$ or $x = -\left(\frac{4}{3}\right)$
25. 20

Challenge Problems: Functions—Tables, Graphs, Notation (p. 65)

1. The function f is undefined when $x = -5$.
2. $x = 0$, $x = -4$, or $x = \frac{1}{3}$
3. 7
4. $2x^2 + 11x + 15$
5. $(x + 2)(3x + 7)$

Checking Progress: Functions—Tables, Graphs, Notation (p. 66)

1. Yes
2. any value b such that $b \neq 3$
3. Yes
4. any value b such that $b \neq 5$
5. -22

Practice Answer Keys (cont.)

6. -12
7. 48
8. $x = 2$ or $x = -11$
9. 16
10. $x^2 + 13x$

Practice: Standard Form, Graphing, Slope, and Writing Equations for a Line (p. 71–73)

1. For each linear function below, identify the slope and the y-intercept.

A. $f(x) = -2x + 5$	slope = -2	y-intercept = 5
B. $g(x) = 0.45x - 2$	slope = 0.45	y-intercept = -2
C. $y = \frac{4}{3}x + \frac{2}{5}$	slope = $\frac{4}{3}$	y-intercept = $\frac{2}{5}$
D. $5y = 4x + 1$	slope = $\frac{4}{5}$	y-intercept = $\frac{1}{5}$
E. $h(x) = 5.43x - 8.76$	slope = 5.43	y-intercept = -8.76
F. $g(x) = -\frac{6}{7}x - \frac{4}{5}$	slope = $-\frac{6}{7}$	y-intercept = $-\frac{4}{5}$
G. $f(x) = 2.13x - 5.42$	slope = 2.13	y-intercept = -5.42
H. $y = 5.6 - 3.5x$	slope = -3.5	y-intercept = 5.6
I. $4.5x - y = 7$	slope = 4.5	y-intercept = -7
J. $2y - 8x = 9$	slope = 4	y-intercept = $\frac{9}{2}$
K. $h(x) = -5.4 + 9x$	slope = 9	y-intercept = -5.4

2. Graph each of the linear functions below on your own paper by completing a table and plotting the points on a coordinate plane.

A. $f(x) = -5x - 7$

x	$f(x)$
1	-12
0	-7
-1	-2

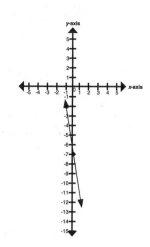

Practice Answer Keys (cont.)

B. $g(x) = \frac{4}{7}x - 9$

x	g(x)
7	-5
0	-9
-7	-13

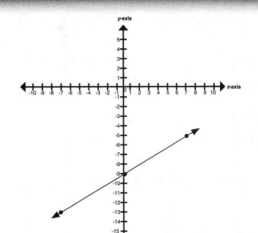

C. $h(x) = -3x + 2$

x	h(x)
1	-1
0	2
-1	5

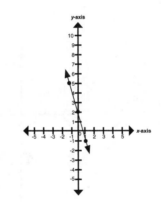

D. $i(x) = \frac{1}{5}x - 4$

x	i(x)
5	-3
0	-4
-5	-5

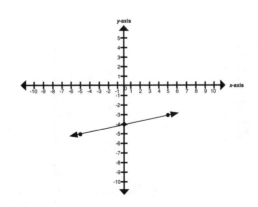

Practice Answer Keys (cont.)

E. $j(x) = 10 - \frac{1}{7}x$

x	j(x)
7	9
0	10
-7	11

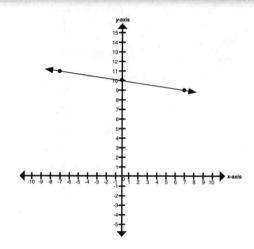

F. $k(x) = -3x - 8$

x	k(x)
1	-11
0	-8
-1	-5

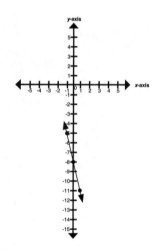

G. $l(x) = 5 - \frac{7}{4}x$

x	l(x)
4	-2
0	5
-4	12

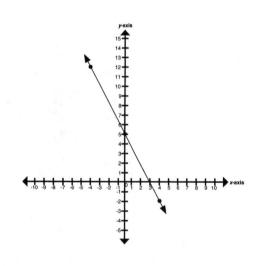

Practice Answer Keys (cont.)

H. $m(x) = -\frac{1}{7}x + 9$

x	m(x)
7	8
0	9
-7	10

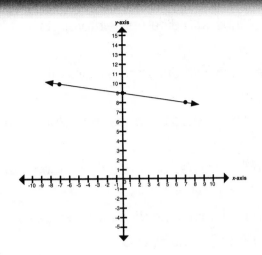

I. $n(x) = 1.5x + 2$

x	n(x)
1	3.9
0	2.4
-1	0.9

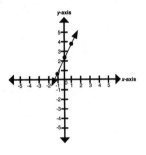

J. $p(x) = -\frac{2}{3}x + 4$

x	p(x)
3	2
0	4
-3	6

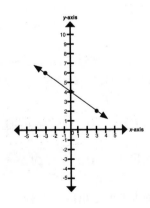

Practice Answer Keys (cont.)

K. They are parallel lines with different *y*-intercepts.

L. Both are -3.

M. They are parallel lines with different *y*-intercepts.

N. Both slopes are $-\frac{1}{7}$.

O. They are perpendicular lines because their slopes are negative reciprocals.

P. Slope of $g(x)$ is $\frac{4}{7}$ and $l(x)$ is $-\frac{7}{4}$.

Q. They are perpendicular lines because their slopes are negative reciprocals.

R. Slope of $f(x)$ is -5 and $i(x)$ is $\frac{1}{5}$.

S. They are perpendicular lines because their slopes are negative reciprocals.

T. Slope of $n(x)$ is 1.5 or $\frac{3}{2}$, and $p(x)$ is $-\frac{2}{3}$.

3.

A. $y = -5x + 27$

B. $y - 12 = \frac{1}{4}(x - 4)$

C. $y - 4 = 3(x - 5)$

D. $y = \frac{2}{3}x + 11$

E. $y = -2x + 17$

F. $y - 0.4 = 9(x + \frac{1}{3})$

G. $y - 2.3 = 3.5(x - 4.5)$

H. $y = \frac{2}{5}x - \frac{3}{5}$

I. $y = -\frac{5}{45}x - \frac{123}{456}$

J. $y + 9 = 0.75(x - 20)$

K. $y - 5 = \frac{9}{2}(x - 2)$

L. $y = \frac{2}{5}x + 18$

4.

A. $16.50

B. $8

C. $9. For this problem, it is assumed that Dave will not have a negative amount of money.

D. This is the money Tanya had before beginning to work.

Challenge Problems: Standard Form, Graphing, Slope, and Writing Equations for a Line (p. 73)

1. Noah is correct because the slope is represented by the coefficient of the *x* term, in this case, it is -2.

2. Jamie is correct because for two lines to be perpendicular, their slopes must be negative reciprocals. The slope of the first line is 4, and the slope of the second line is $-\frac{1}{4}$, which are negative reciprocals of each other.

3. $y = 5x - 44$

Practice Answer Keys (cont.)

Checking Progress: Standard Form, Graphing, Slope, and Writing Equations for a Line (p. 74)

1. For each linear function below, identify the slope and the *y*-intercept.

A. $f(x) = -7x + 2$	slope = -7	*y*-intercept = 2
B. $g(x) = -\frac{1}{4}x - \frac{2}{87}$	slope = $-\frac{1}{4}$	*y*-intercept = $-\frac{2}{87}$
C. $y = 0.54x + 0.45$	slope = 0.54	*y*-intercept = 0.45

2.

A. $f(x) = -3x + 2$

x	$f(x)$
1	-1
0	2
-1	5

B. $g(x) = -\frac{5}{4}x - 1$

x	$g(x)$
4	-6
0	-1
-4	4

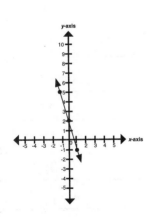

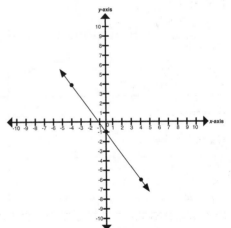

C. $h(x) = \frac{1}{3}x + 9$

x	$h(x)$
3	10
0	9
-3	8

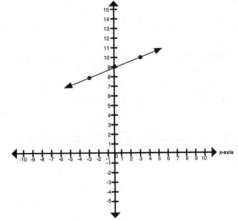

Practice Answer Keys (cont.)

D. $p(x) = -\frac{5}{4}x + 14$

x	$p(x)$
4	9
0	14
-4	19

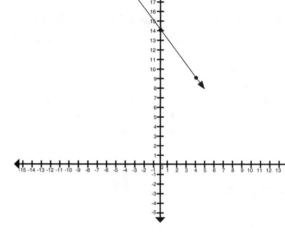

E. They are perpendicular lines.

F. Slope of $f(x)$ is -3 and $h(x)$ is $\frac{1}{3}$.

G. They are parallel lines.

H. Slope of both is $-\frac{5}{4}$.

3.

A. $y = -\frac{3}{2}x + \frac{15}{16}$

B. $y - 9 = 1.2(x - 15)$

C. $y - 3 = -(x - 4)$

D. $y = \frac{1}{3}x + \frac{31}{3}$

Practice: Quadratic Functions (p. 78–79)

1.

Function	Parabola Opens	y-intercept
A. $f(x) = 3x^2$	Up	(0, 0)
B. $g(x) = -\frac{1}{2}x^2 - 2x + 1$	Down	(0, 1)
C. $h(x) = 4x^2 + 10x$	Up	(0, 0)
D. $f(x) = 0.23x^2 - 0.5x + 1$	Up	(0, 1)
E. $g(x) = \frac{1}{5}x^2 + 5$	Up	(0, 5)
F. $h(x) = -0.45x^2 - 0.24x + 0.1$	Down	(0, 0.1)
G. $f(x) = 2x^2 + 7$	Up	(0, 7)
H. $g(x) = \frac{3}{7}x^2 - \frac{4}{5}x + \frac{1}{3}$	Up	$(0, \frac{1}{3})$
I. $h(x) = -\frac{5}{9}x^2$	Down	(0, 0)
J. $f(x) = 0.75x^2 - 3x + \frac{2}{9}$	Up	$(0, \frac{2}{9})$
K. $g(x) = -12x^2 + 21$	Down	(0, 21)

Practice Answer Keys (cont.)

2.

A. $(1, 7)$

B. $(-\frac{1}{6}, -6\frac{1}{12})$

C. $(0, 0)$

D. $(0, \frac{1}{2})$

E. $(\frac{3}{8}, \frac{153}{16})$

F. $(1, -1)$

G. $(\frac{1}{5}, 3\frac{1}{5})$

H $(-\frac{3}{8}, -\frac{393}{64})$

I. $(-0.75, -\frac{119}{32})$

J. $(-0.05, 0.505)$

K. $(0, \frac{8}{3})$

3.

A. None

B. $(-\frac{1}{6} + \sqrt{73}, 0)$ and $(-\frac{1}{6} - \sqrt{73}, 0)$

C. $(0, 0)$

D. $\left(\frac{\sqrt{0.4}}{0.4}, 0\right)$ and $\left(\frac{-\sqrt{0.4}}{0.4}, 0\right)$; or $\left(\frac{5\sqrt{10}}{10}, 0\right)$ and $\left(\frac{-5\sqrt{10}}{10}, 0\right)$

E. $\left(\frac{3}{10}, 0\right)$ and $\left(-\frac{12}{7}, 0\right)$

F. $(2, 0)$ and $(0, 0)$

G. $\left(-\frac{8}{3}, 0\right)$ and $\left(\frac{5}{4}, 0\right)$

H. $\left(\frac{-\frac{3}{8} + \sqrt{393}}{8}\right)$ and $\left(\frac{\frac{3}{8} - \sqrt{393}}{8}\right)$

Practice Answer Keys (cont.)

I. (-10, 0) and (20, 0)

J. $\left(\dfrac{\frac{1}{20} + \sqrt{101}}{20}\right)$ and $\left(\dfrac{\frac{-1}{20} - \sqrt{101}}{20}\right)$

K. $\left(-\frac{2}{3}, 0\right)$ and $\left(\frac{8}{9}, 0\right)$

4. The vertex is (0, 4), and it does not have any *x*-intercepts. However, two other points are (1, 7) and (-1, 7), and a third point can be easily found.

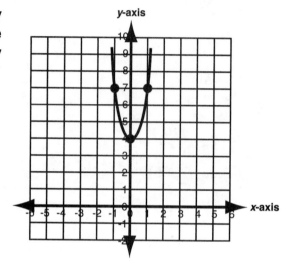

5. The vertex is $\left(-\frac{3}{2}, \frac{37}{4}\right)$, and two other points are (1, 3) and (-1, 9).

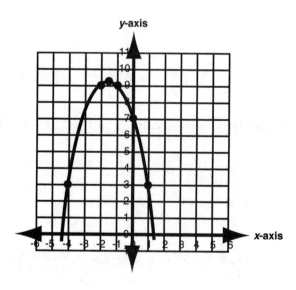

Practice Answer Keys (cont.)

6. The vertex is (-2, -10), and two other points are
    (0, -8) and (-4, -8).

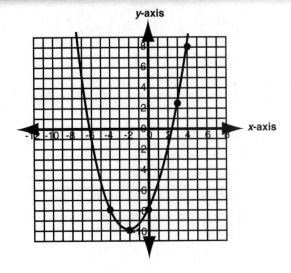

7. The vertex is $\left(-\frac{3}{8}, \frac{9}{16}\right)$, and two other points are
    (0, 0) and (-1, -1).

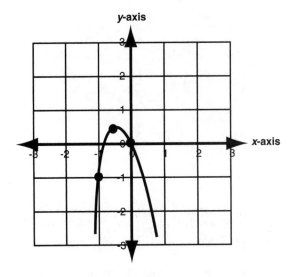

Challenge Problems: Quadratic Functions (p. 80)

1. Yanta needs to look at the coefficient, *a*, of the x^2 term. If *a* is positive, then the parabola opens up, and if *a* is negative, then the parabola opens down. If *a* is greater than one, in absolute value, the parabola is considered narrow; if *a* is less than one, in absolute value, the parabola is considered wide.

2. Katie is correct because she has the correct *y* value for the vertex.

3. Neelie is correct because the determinant is less than 0.

Practice Answer Keys (cont.)

4. Vertex: $\left(-\frac{73}{120}, -\frac{529}{2400}\right)$; x-intercepts: $\left(-\frac{5}{12}, 0\right)$ and $\left(\frac{2}{25}, 0\right)$; opens up and is a narrow parabola.

Checking Progress: Quadratic Functions (p. 81)

1.

Function	Parabola Opens	Narrow or Wide
A. $f(x) = -x^2 - 5$	Down	Neither
B. $g(x) = 1.75x^2 - 3x + 4$	Up	Narrow
C. $h(x) = -\frac{1}{4}x^2 + 23x$	Down	Wide

2.

A. $\left(-\frac{5}{6}, \frac{49}{12}\right)$

B. $\left(-\frac{16}{55}, -\frac{8864}{1375}\right)$

C. $\left(-\frac{4}{3}, \frac{97}{117}\right)$

3.

A. $\left(\frac{2}{5}, 0\right)$ and $\left(\frac{5}{9}, 0\right)$

B. None

C. $(6, 0)$ and $(-7, 0)$

4. The vertex is $\left(-\frac{1}{2}, -\frac{25}{4}\right)$, and the x-intercepts are $(2, 0)$ and $(-3, 0)$. Another point is $(0, -6)$.

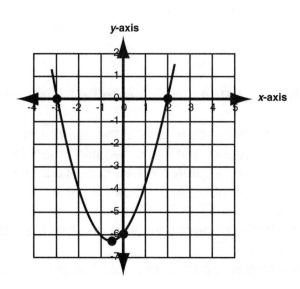

Check-Up Problems Answer Keys

Check-Up Problems: Number Systems (p. 82)

1. rational, real
2. irrational, real
3. whole, integer, rational, real
4. whole, integer, rational, real
5. irrational, real
6. rational, real
7. rational, real
8. whole, integer, rational, real
9. integer, rational, real
10. none

Check-Up Problems: Properties (p. 83)

1. 512
2. 253
3. $19b$
4. $49z + 32a$
5. Compute as $961 + 39 = 1,000$; $1,000 + 872 = 1,872$
6. $50 \cdot 2 = 100$; $100 \cdot 792,234 = 79,223,400$
7. Compute as $25 + 5 = 30$; $13 \cdot 30 = 390$
8. Note that $2\frac{1}{3} = \frac{7}{3}$; $\frac{7}{3} \cdot \frac{3}{7} = 1$; $1 \cdot 15 = 15$.
9. $c^2(431c^3 + 29)$
10. Commutative Property of Multiplication

Check-Up Problems: Exponents and Exponential Expressions (p. 84)

1. 0.00032
2. -27
3. 21
4. 6,400
5. 1,000
6. $-3a^2 - 7b^4$
7. $11a^2 - 7b^4$
8. $a^{49} \cdot b^{128}$
9. $\dfrac{-1}{(2)^4} = -\frac{1}{16} = -0.0625$
10. y^{420}

Check-Up Problems Answer Keys (cont.)

Check-Up Problems: Roots and Radicals (p. 85)

1. 105
2. 31
3. $12z^{12}$
4. a^8z^8
5. $2^7 \cdot 7^2 \cdot 13\sqrt{2 \cdot 13}$
6. $11\sqrt{30}$
7. $\frac{1}{4}\sqrt{26}$
8. $\frac{3}{8}\sqrt{2}$
9. $12\sqrt{3z}$
10. $(30z^4 - 42z)\sqrt{5z}$

Check-up: Operations on Algebraic Expressions (p. 86)

1. $31a + 10.7y$
2. $3.01x + 0.17y$
3. $\frac{85}{8}x$
4. $0.093x^3z^4$
5. $\frac{2x^3yz^2}{5} = 0.4x^3yz^2$
6. $\frac{49x^3}{9z^2w}$
7. 24
8. $\frac{1}{2}$
9. $\frac{292}{385}$
10. $15x$

Check-up: Equations and Problem Solving (p. 87)

1. $6x^2 - x - 2 = 0$
2. $x = 2.5$ or $x = -7$
3. $x = -11$ or $x = 3$
4. $x = 1$ or $x = 5$
5. $x = 1.5$ or $x = -4$
6. $x = 6$ or $x = -3$
7. $x = 1$ or $x = -\frac{2}{3}$
8. The length of the rectangle is 22 cm, and the width is 17 cm.

Check-Up Problems Answer Keys (cont.)

9. $(2a + 5)(b - 2)$
10. $x = -1 + \sqrt{3}$, or $x = -1 - \sqrt{3}$

Check-up: Graphing (p. 88)

1. IV
2. $y = 0$
3. IV
4. $(2, 2)$
5. $(1, -4)$, $(2, -3)$, $(3, -2)$, and $(4, -1)$
6–10. See graph at right.

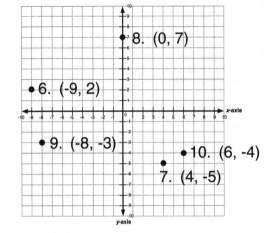

Check-up: Functions (p. 89–90)

1. No
2. 3
3. No
4. 5
5. 8
6. 18
7. -12
8. $x = 1$ or $x = 8$
9. $x = -2$
10. $x^2 - 5x - 6$

Check-up: Linear Functions (p. 91)

1.

A. $f(x) = -12x - \frac{31}{5}$	slope = -12	y-intercept = $-\frac{31}{5}$
B. $g(x) = -2.35x - 3.46$	slope = -2.35	y-intercept = -3.46
C. $y = \frac{1}{3}x + 18$	slope = $\frac{1}{3}$	y-intercept = 18

2. A. $g(x) = \frac{2}{3}x + 8$

x	$g(x)$
3	10
0	8
-3	6

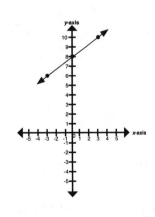

Check-Up Problems Answer Keys (cont.)

B. $h(x) = \frac{5}{11}x - 1$

x	h(x)
11	4
0	-1
-11	-6

C. $f(x) = -2.2x - 4$

x	f(x)
5	-15
0	-4
-5	7

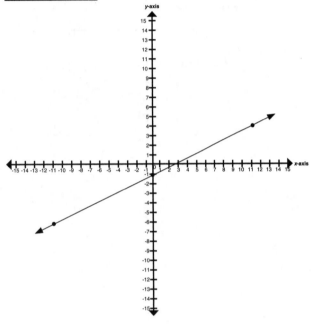

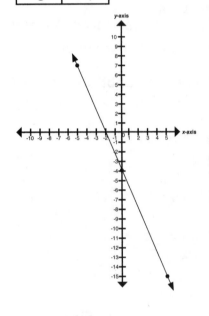

D. $p(x) = \frac{2}{3}x - 3$

x	p(x)
3	-1
0	-3
-3	-5

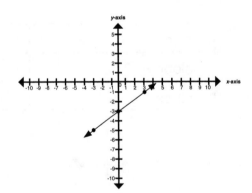

E. They are perpendicular lines.

F. The slope of $f(x)$ is -2.2 or $-\frac{11}{5}$ and $h(x)$ is $\frac{5}{11}$.

G. They are parallel lines.

H. The slope of $g(x)$ is $\frac{2}{3}$ and $p(x)$ is $\frac{2}{3}$.

Check-Up Problems Answer Keys (cont.)

3. Write the equation for the line that satisfies the given information.

A. $y = -\frac{5}{12}x + \frac{14}{13}$

B. $y + 8 = -3(x - 2)$

C. $y + 2 = -\frac{1}{2}(x + 2)$

D. $y = -x - 12$

Check-up: Quadratic Functions (p. 92)

1.

Function	Parabola Opens	Narrow or Wide
A. $f(x) = 2x^2 - 3$	Up	Narrow
B. $g(x) = -3.2x^2 + 23.45x$	Down	Narrow
C. $h(x) = \frac{2}{3}x^2 - \frac{5}{67}x + 2.1$	Up	Wide

2. A. $\left(\frac{39}{41}, \frac{4791}{205}\right)$

B. $\left(\frac{3}{20}, \frac{579}{700}\right)$

C. $\left(-\frac{5}{6}, \frac{433}{12}\right)$

3. A. $\left(-\frac{11}{8}, 0\right)$ and $\left(-\frac{13}{6}, 0\right)$

B. None

C. $\left(\frac{16}{9}, 0\right)$ and $\left(\frac{10}{9}, 0\right)$

4. The vertex is (-5, 0) which is also the x-intercept. Two other points are (-7, 4) and (-4, 1).

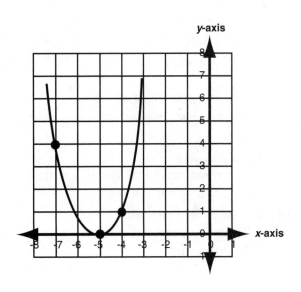

References

References

Brown, R., Dolciani, M., Sorgenfrey, R., Cole, W., (1997). *Algebra structure and method book 1.* Evanston, IL: McDougal Littell.

Chicago Mathematics Project (found online July 2004). *Connected mathematics.* University of Chicago. Found online at: http://www.math.msu.edu/cmp/curriculum/Algebra.htm

Edwards, E. (1990). *Algebra for everyone.* Reston, VA: National Council of Teachers of Mathematics.

Long, L. (1998). *Painless algebra.* Hauppauge, NY: Barron's Educational Series.

National Council of Teachers of Mathematics (NCTM). (2000). *Principles and standards for school mathematics.* Reston, VA: National Council of Teachers of Mathematics.

National Council of Teachers of Mathematics (NCTM). (2004). *Standards and expectations for algebra.* Reston, VA: National Council of Teachers of Mathematics. Found online at: http://www.nctm.org

Freudenthal Institute at the University of Utrecht / University of Wisconsin / NSF (found online July 2004) *Math in context.* http://www.showmecenter.missouri.edu/showme/mic.shtml Encyclopedia Britannica.

Web Resources

About Math
http://math.about.com/od/quadraticequation/
http://math.about.com/gi/dynamic/offsite.htm?site=http%3A%2F%2Fwww.hyper-ad.com%2Ftutoring%2Fmath%2Falgebra%2FComplete_square.html

Algebra.help. (2001–2004)
http://www.algebrahelp.com/index.jsp

Algebra Solutions
http://www.gomath.com/algebra.html

Awesome Library—Algebra
http://www.awesomelibrary.org/Classroom/Mathematics/Middle-High_School_Math/Algebra.html

References (cont.)

Borenson, H. (2001–2004) *Hands on Equations.* Allentown, PA: Borenson and Associates.
Found online at: http://www.borenson.com/?src=overture

Brennon, J. (2002) *Understanding algebra.*
Found online at: http://www.jamesbrennan.org/algebra/

Classzone Algebra 1
http://www.classzone.com/books/algebra_1/index.cfm

College Algebra Home Page West Texas A & M University
http://www.wtamu.edu/academic/anns/mps/math/mathlab/col_algebra/index.htm
http://www.wtamu.edu/academic/anns/mps/math/mathlab/col_algebra/col_alg_tut15_rateq.htm

Cool Math Sites
http://www.cte.jhu.edu/techacademy/web/2000/heal/mathsites.htm

Ed Helper.com
http://www.edhelper.com/algebra.htm

History of Algebra
http://www.ucs.louisiana.edu/~sxw8045/history.htm

Holt, Rinehart, and Winston Mathematics in Context
http://www.hrw.com/math/mathincontext/index.htm

Interactive Mathematic Miscellany and Puzzles
http://www.cut-the-knot.org/algebra.shtml

Introduction to Algebra
http://www.mathleague.com/help/algebra/algebra.htm

Math Archives: Topics in Mathematics, Algebra
http://www.archives.math.utk.edu/topics/algebra.html

Moses, B. *The algebra project.* Cambridge, MA: The Algebra Project, Inc.
http://www.algebra.org/index.html

Oracle Education Foundation Think Quest Library (2004) Algebra
Found online at: http://library.thinkquest.org/10030/algecon.htm

References (cont.)

Purple Math
    http://www.purplemath.com/modules/solvrtnl.htm

Reichman, H. and Kohn, M. (2004) *Math made easy.*
    Found online at: http://mathmadeeasy.com/algebra.html

Reliable problem solving in all subjects that use mathematics for problem solving. Algebra, Physics, Chemistry... from grade school to grad school and beyond.
    http://www2.hawaii.edu/suremath/intro_algebra.html

Show Me Center
    http://www.showmecenter.missouri.edu/showme/

SOS Mathematics
    http://www.sosmath.com/
    http://www.sosmath.com/algebra/quadraticeq/complsquare/complsquare.html

Surfing the Net With Kids
    http://www.surfnetkids.com/algebra.htm

The Math Forum Drexel University (1994–2004) K–12 Internet Algebra Resources. Philadelphia, PA.
    http://mathforum.org/algebra/k12.algebra.html

University of Akron Theoretical and Applied Mathematics
    http://www.math.uakron.edu/~dpstory/mpt_home.html

Real Life Applications of Math

Applied Academics: Applications of Mathematics—Careers
    http://www.bced.gov.bc.ca/careers/aa/lessons/math.htm

Exactly How is Math Used in Technology?
    http://www.math.bcit.ca/examples/index.shtml

Mathematics Association of America—Careers
    http://www.maa.org/careers/index.html

NASA Space Link
    http://www.spacelink.msfc.nasa.gov/.index.html